ACHIEVING
NEXT GENERATION
LITERACY

ACHIEVING NEXT GENERATION LITERACY

Using the Tests (You Think) You Hate
to Help the Students You Love

MAUREEN CONNOLLY   VICKY GIOUROUKAKIS

Alexandria, Virginia USA

1703 N. Beauregard St. • Alexandria, VA 22311-1714 USA
Phone: 800-933-2723 or 703-578-9600 • Fax: 703-575-5400
Website: www.ascd.org • E-mail: member@ascd.org
Author guidelines: www.ascd.org/write

Deborah S. Delisle, *Executive Director;* Robert D. Clouse, *Managing Director, Digital Content & Publications;* Stefani Roth, *Publisher;* Genny Ostertag, *Director, Content Acquisitions;* Julie Houtz, *Director, Book Editing & Production;* Katie Martin, *Editor;* Thomas Lytle, *Senior Graphic Designer;* Mike Kalyan, *Manager, Production Services;* Cynthia Stock, *Typesetter;* Kelly Marshall, *Senior Production Specialist*

All referenced trademarks are the property of their respective owners. Florida Standards Assessments (FSA) content appears by permission of the Florida Department of Education, Office of K–12 Assessment, Tallahassee, Florida 32399-0400. The Massachusetts Comprehensive Assessment System (MCAS) item is included by permission of the Massachusetts Department of Elementary and Secondary Education. Inclusion does not constitute endorsement of this book or any other commercial publication. MCAS sample student responses are posted at http://www.doe.mass.edu/mcas/student/.

All web links in this book are correct as of the publication date below but may have become inactive or otherwise modified since that time. If you notice a deactivated or changed link, please e-mail books@ascd.org with the words "Link Update" in the subject line. In your message, please specify the web link, the book title, and the page number on which the link appears.

PAPERBACK ISBN: 978-1-4166-2163-8   ASCD product #116023   n6/16
PDF E-BOOK ISBN: 978-1-4166-2259-8; see Books in Print for other formats.
Quantity discounts: 10–49, 10%; 50+, 15%; 1,000+, special discounts
(e-mail programteam@ascd.org or call 800-933-2723, ext. 5773, or 703-575-5773).
For desk copies, go to www.ascd.org/deskcopy.

Library of Congress Cataloging-in-Publication Data
Names: Connolly, Maureen (English teacher), author. | Giouroukakis, Vicky, author.
Title: Achieving next generation literacy : using the tests (you think) you hate to help the students you love / Maureen Connolly, Vicky Giouroukakis.
Description: Alexandria, VA : ASCD, 2016. | Includes bibliographical references and index.
Identifiers: LCCN 2016001290 | ISBN 9781416621638 (pbk.)
Subjects: LCSH: Language arts (Secondary)—United States. | Language arts—Correlation with content subjects. | Content area reading. | Critical thinking. | Language arts (Secondary)—Standards—United States. | Common Core State Standards (Education)
Classification: LCC LB1631 .C6598 2016 | DDC 428.0071/2—dc23 LC record available at http://lccn.loc.gov/2016001290

25 24 23 22 21 20 19 18 17 16   1 2 3 4 5 6 7 8 9 10 11 12

✦ ✦ ✦

We dedicate this book to all the teachers who commit themselves to being the best that they can be in order to make a difference in children's lives. They know that their tireless efforts are more important than teacher rating scores and that student development and understanding are more important than test scores.

ACHIEVING NEXT GENERATION LITERACY

Acknowledgments

We wish to thank Carol Chambers Collins and the entire ASCD staff, in particular Katie Martin, for their belief in our vision for this book and for their continued support of this product from start to finish. We would also like to thank our colleagues at our respective institutions of education—The College of New Jersey in Ewing, New Jersey, and Molloy College in Rockville Centre, New York—for their sustained encouragement of our work, especially the ELA professionals with whom we have worked over the years who have inspired us. In addition, we wish to express our gratitude to the students we have taught in the past and will teach in the future for motivating us to become better teachers. Finally, we would like to sincerely thank all those who work tirelessly to ensure quality education for all students.

A very special acknowledgment goes to our families—Maureen's husband, Andrew, and children, Ben and Anna Rose, and Vicky's husband, John, and children, Emanuel, Anna, and Paul—for their unwavering love, patience, and encouragement.

Introduction: It's Not About Teaching to the Test

Let's start with a question. Who do you think said the following?

> We firmly believe that rates of college and career readiness and postsecondary success will not improve if teachers and students are distracted by the need to speed through impossibly broad course content and spend time on narrowly cast test preparation in an understandable but misguided effort to boost scores at the expense of mastery of critical knowledge, skills, and understandings.

Sounds like a parent or a teacher speaking out against test-prep culture, doesn't it? We thought so, too. Actually, these are the words of the College Board (2014c, p. 14), and they fuel our hope that the redesign of the SAT and the upcoming tests from the Partnership for Assessment of Readiness for College and Careers (PARCC) and the Smarter Balanced Assessment Consortium (Smarter Balanced) will reflect the belief that test prep should not replace deeper learning.

The quote from the College Board is so good that we need to share the rest of it:

> Further, we believe that the rates of college and career readiness and postsecondary success will improve only if our nation's teachers are empowered to help the full range of students practice the kinds of rigorous, engaging daily work through which academic excellence can genuinely and reliably be attained. (College Board, 2014c, p. 12)

That is what this book is about: teaching rich and challenging content in engaging ways that will equip students for postsecondary success while still preparing them to be successful on high-stakes exams—whether the SAT or ACT, achievement tests from PARCC and Smarter Balanced, or independent state assessments.

What Do Our Students Really Need?

We are living in an age in which a test score is assumed to reflect the quality of the instruction a student has received. But if we were to really consider what the indicators of a good education are, we would come up with many different answers representing a range of values and viewpoints. The conversation might go on for hours. Because this is a book focused on literacy, the question can be narrowed a bit: *What are the markers of an effective literacy education? What do our students really need in order to be literate? What are the qualities that a literate individual possesses?*

Here's what we believe literate individuals are able to do:

1. **Demonstrate independence** with complex text by asking questions and being able to clarify information.

2. **Build strong content knowledge** through purposeful reading, writing, viewing, listening, and research.

3. **Respond to varying demands of audience, task, purpose, and discipline** by shifting tone and selecting convincing evidence.

4. **Comprehend as well as critique** by analyzing the content and bias of sources.

5. **Value evidence** in arguments they hear, read, or develop.

6. Use technology strategically and capably by integrating sources and using tools to support their intentions.

7. Come to understand other perspectives and cultures through evaluation of their own perspectives and the perspectives of others.

If these qualities look familiar, it's because they are the seven "capacities of the literate individual" (CLI) outlined in the Common Core State Standards for English Language Arts (ELA) & Literacy in History/Social Studies, Science, and Technical Subjects (Common Core State Standards Initiative [CCSSI], 2015). Although the Common Core State Standards remain controversial for a number of reasons, we hope you will agree that the capacities described are ones that all students should develop. We believe that they are important life skills, critical to the exercise of the rights and responsibilities of global citizens and to the navigation of everyday life. Together, they form a portrait of what we are calling "next generation literacy."

The Common Core State Standards for ELA and content area literacy have been designed to ensure students will be college and career ready in terms of reading, writing, speaking and listening, and language skills. Although the stated purpose of these standards is to prepare students to engage in the *processes* that are necessary in the college classroom or in the workforce, ironically, it's not the processes but the *products* of the Common Core (test scores) that tend to preoccupy educators, students, and parents. Throughout this text, the product we focus on is not test scores but students' acquisition and development of the capacities of the literate individual. To frame this in terms of the "backward design" model of lesson planning popularized by Grant Wiggins and Jay McTighe (2005), the CLI are the desired results, and the various high-stakes tests students must take provide evidence of those desired results.

Of course, we want to focus on the practical, so the next question we need to ask is this: *What can we do in the classroom to help students develop the capacities of the literate individual and achieve next generation literacy?*

Teaching *Informed* by the Tests

One of the dangers of standards-based assessments is teachers thinking that they need to narrow their rich curricula and gear their instruction toward testing. Perhaps they incorporate fewer, if any, creative activities like role-play and reader's theater; perhaps they devote more time to drills, rote memorization, and practice exams. While these approaches can help students become more comfortable with high-stakes exams, they also send the harmful message that exams are the end-all, be-all of education . . . that test scores are more important than the process of learning. By contrast, in the authentic type of classroom most teachers strive for, the focus is helping students acquire the knowledge and skills that will help them succeed on a much broader scale.

    To write this book, we pored over sample test questions from PARCC, Smarter Balanced, the SAT and ACT, and representative state standards-based exams, and then we connected the content of these questions with the CLI. Our hope is that after reading this book, you will teach with these capacities as a primary concern and look to the tests your students will take as a resource for helping them develop the skills and knowledge they need.

Who We Are

Together, we have more than 25 years of teaching experience at the high school level. Both of us made the transition from teaching high school to teaching preservice and inservice secondary education teachers at the undergraduate and graduate levels. We've collaborated several times as writers, always keeping our focus on providing practical advice to our colleagues in the field. Both of the books we have published together (Giouroukakis & Connolly,

2012, 2013) help the reader navigate the most efficient route to creating standards-based lessons that optimize student learning.

Maureen has a passion for service learning, so throughout this book, you will note many lessons that relate to social issues. Vicky is an expert at developing strategies to meet the needs of English language learners (ELLs) and struggling learners. She made sure that all the strategies we recommend throughout the text include clear and simple ways that they can be used to differentiate instruction. Whenever we choose information to include in the lessons we present to preservice and inservice teachers and whenever we write professional materials, we always ask ourselves, "Is this information clear and transferable into most classrooms?" Only when the answer is "yes" do we share it. The contents of this book meet that same standard of practicality.

As teacher educators, we are constantly trying to examine our own practice and reflect on what is working and what needs development. Backward design provides a framework for our planning, and we use the Common Core State Standards in general, and the CLI in particular, to guide our thinking about enduring understandings, skills, knowledge, and transfer. Although the Common Core State Standards have encouraged us to focus more on expository text and argument, we want to stress that novels, poetry, and short stories, along with narrative and creative writing, still hold an essential place in students' literacy development.

Who This Book Is For

This book is for you! We are writing for middle and high school–level English language arts professionals (teachers, administrators, literacy coaches, staff developers, and teacher educators in the field of ELA) who recognize they need to prepare students for the next generation of exams but want to do so in a way that engages students in content learning and the development of next generation literacy and critical thinking skills.

What This Book Is For

In the pages ahead, we focus on the capacities of the literate individual, illustrate what the next generation of assessments that are designed to measure these CLI look like, and explore the knowledge and skills these tests require. Then we show you how to use the backward design model to create rich and challenging lessons that are aligned with the tests and incorporate the strategies you need to foster student success.

We want to be clear that this is *not* a test-prep book. We have no interest in drill-and-kill practices that narrow learning just to get students to pass an exam. This is a book about engaging, meaningful instructional methods and strategies for developing students' literacy skills and showing students how to transfer those skills to success on assessments. It is a resource for ELA professionals that provides answers to the questions so many of today's teachers have:

• *How can I prepare my students for standardized testing without sacrificing the creativity and passion for learning that are true to my values and to the ideals of the profession?*

• *How can I provide student-centered instructional methods and activities that are standards-based, engaging, motivating, thought-provoking, and meaningful—and that will also translate to high test scores?*

How This Book Is Organized

The book is divided into two parts. In Part I, we make overt the ways that test development reflects literacy skills and influences instruction. Chapter 1 addresses the question of what it means to be literate in the 21st century and explores the literacy capacities that we want our students to have by the time they graduate from high school. Then we discuss how backward design can provide a roadmap for developing the CLI students need to succeed on exams and, more critically, also need to succeed in college, in their careers, and throughout their lives as involved, interested, and interesting human beings.

In Chapter 2, we analyze the next generation of exams and discuss the mindful literacy-focused changes made to the SAT exam as well as the development of the newer standards-based tests from the two national testing consortia, PARCC and Smarter Balanced. We also analyze various state tests. We compare similar components shared by these exams and highlight the unique qualities of each. We make purposeful connections among the components of the exams and specific CLI so that you can consider knowledge and skills that you want your students to develop.

In Part II, covering Chapters 3–8, we explore six of the seven CLI, highlighting each one's component skills and modeling the process of creating lessons that will help students develop mastery. Note that we do not include a chapter for the first capacity—*demonstrate independence with complex text by asking questions and clarifying information,* which encompasses the many ways that we want students to be independent in their reading, writing, speaking and listening, and language. It's the development of the other six capacities that makes this kind of independence possible. Each chapter in Part II also presents a sample lesson for one of the capacities, and every lesson has a strong focus on differentiation. The chapters in Part II present dozens of instructional strategies (42 in total), and in the book's Conclusion you will find a master chart that captures all the strategies associated with each capacity (see pp. 135–136).

Neither effective instruction nor this book is about teaching to the tests. Ultimately, the approach we advocate underscores that meaningful learning experiences are about enabling student growth and self-sufficiency. It's our hope you will consult this book for new ideas and practical strategies for fostering your students' development as independent, literate, well-educated individuals who are *also* well prepared to ace their high-stakes tests.

PART I

A Time of Change

The Next Generation of Literate Individuals and Assessments

In this section, we delve more deeply into the capacities of the literate individual (CLI) and analyze sample test items from the next generation assessments (SAT, ACT, PARCC, Smarter Balanced, and various state tests). Our intention is to encourage you to consider what is most important for students to learn as they work to become literate individuals and how these new assessments reflect the skills and knowledge we want students to develop. The figures and analysis we present highlight both the similarities among the various tests and the connections between these tests and the CLI. As we state in the Introduction, we want to focus primarily on students' development as literate individuals and only secondarily on test preparation. If students have developed the CLI, they will be successful on exams.

This part of the book provides a lens through which to examine the lesson design process, learning experiences, and strategies covered in Part II. With a clear understanding of the CLI and the means by which tests strive to measure students' progress in the development of these capacities, you'll be prepared to make better-informed instructional decisions.

1

What Is a Literate Individual?

Being a literate person today means more than being able to read and write. In a world diverse with cultures, print texts, media, and technologies, a literate person needs to possess certain specific capabilities.

Let's think about the daily literacy-related practices of a typical adolescent (we'll call him Paul).

Paul wakes up to the sound of his smartphone's alarm. He picks it up and checks the time. Then he reads and responds to any e-mails and text messages that came in overnight. A game or two on his screen may tempt him to stay on his phone a bit longer. Paul goes on Facebook, scrolls through his friends' statuses, "liking" and commenting, and then posts a status of his own. Instagram is next, where he looks at his friends' pictures, comments, and maybe posts a picture or two saved on his phone. Then Paul fires up his tablet, drops in on a few different websites, and scans the day's headlines to catch up on the news and last night's scores.

Both in school and while doing his homework, Paul uses digital tools and devices to complete assignments. He navigates the Internet to locate reliable websites for information and reads a diverse variety of online texts—some that he finds or chooses himself, and others that are provided or curated by his teachers. As his teachers require, Paul synthesizes the information he finds, identifying text-based evidence that he'll go on to cite, and he selects the product format best suited for his goals (e.g., a multimedia presentation, a short digital movie, a wiki, role-play, a discussion, an essay). He shares his work with an audience of diverse peers, some of whom are just learning English, some of whom come from cultural backgrounds very different from his own, some of whom seem to learn much more easily than he does, and some of whom are pursuing goals set out for them in individual education plans. Paul and his classmates give feedback on one another's work and share their takes on classroom content in all kinds of learning arrangements, from partner work to small groups to the whole class. His after-school circle is similarly diverse—all kinds of kids meeting up in person or online to explore and pursue expertise in sports, music, gaming, and other areas of interest. Paul's life is all about taking in information, reflecting on it, sharing it, connecting with others, and communicating about what he's seen, read, thought about, experienced, and felt.

How does this portrait connect with what it means to be a student who meets rigorous academic standards and is college and career ready? An expanded overview of the seven capacities of the literate individual (CLI), paraphrased from their presentation in the Common Core State Standards (CCSSI, 2015), will shed some light on how Paul exhibits next generation literacy.

1. Literate individuals demonstrate independence with text. They can, independently, with little guidance from teachers and peers, comprehend varied, complex print and digital texts, communicate and build on others' ideas, and understand and apply academic and discipline-specific vocabulary and conventions of English. They know how to use strategies and employ them when necessary to comprehend texts and apply literacy knowledge and skills.

2. Literate individuals build strong content knowledge. They acquire and share knowledge of subject matter through reading, writing, and speaking as well as research and study. They read and understand discipline-specific texts and become experts in the content.

3. Literate individuals respond to varying demands of audience, task, purpose, and discipline. They set and adjust their communication in relation to audience, task, purpose, and discipline. They understand how words affect meaning in writing and in speech, depending on the audience and the purpose, and how different disciplines call for providing different types of evidence.

4. Literate individuals comprehend as well as critique. They understand and can explain what writers, speakers, and visual and mixed media creators are saying through their texts, but they also know how to analyze and examine these texts critically. They question an author's assumptions and biases and evaluate the veracity and logical reasoning of the claims.

5. Literate individuals value evidence. They can cite evidence to support their interpretation of text, both verbally and in writing. They also communicate their reasoning effectively and know how to evaluate the reasoning and arguments of others.

6. Literate individuals use technology and digital media strategically and capably. They employ technology thoughtfully and effectively and can determine which media are best suited for their communication goals. They also synthesize information found through various media and technologies.

7. Literate individuals come to understand other perspectives and cultures. They encounter perspectives and ways of life that are different from their own through reading, writing, and listening, and they are able to work and communicate effectively with peers of diverse backgrounds. Through reading multicultural literature, they have new experiences that expand their cultural understanding and sensitivity.

What can teachers do to help their students acquire, develop, and refine the capacities of the literate individual? We can keep these CLI at the forefront of our thinking during planning. Backward design can help with this. Read on!

Using Backward Design as a Planning Framework

When it comes to lesson planning, many teachers, especially the preservice teachers whom we teach in college, tend to focus a lot on their *inputs*—what they and the students will *do* and *say* during a lesson. They focus a lot less on the *outcomes* they want to see as a result of students' learning experiences. Backward design is a curricular design approach that puts outcomes, otherwise known as the lesson goals, at the forefront, then has the teacher work "backward" to plan the learning experiences that will help students achieve these goals. In the end, backward design provides a roadmap teachers can use to guide students to the intended destination—mastery of particular skills, objectives, or, in our case, CLI. It calls for teachers to consider the "big ideas" in the content they are delivering and then frame them around "essential questions."

First introduced by Grant Wiggins and Jay McTighe in 1998 and then revised and expanded in 2005, backward design consists of three stages:

• **Stage 1: Identify desired results.** Teachers decide on the essential understandings, knowledge, and skills that they want their students to gain as a result of the curriculum. For our purposes, the desired results are one or more of the CLI.

• **Stage 2: Determine acceptable evidence.** Next, teachers create or choose formal and informal assessments that will generate evidence of students' developing knowledge and understanding. In this stage, the questions are "How will students show me they are moving toward mastery of the CLI? How will I ask them to reflect upon and assess their learning?" We can use a variety of measurement instruments—everything from high-stakes tests to traditional unit-ending exams to authentic, performance-based tasks and assignments—to identify and document students' literacy development.

• **Stage 3: Plan learning experiences and instruction.** Finally, teachers plan and design learning experiences and teaching that will enable students to achieve the desired results. In Stage 3, the focus turns more explicitly to inputs: "What activities, instruction, sources, and methods will promote my students' understanding, interest, and excellence in the identified capacity?"

Figure 1.1 shows a backward design approach to developing the capacities of the literate individual.

FIGURE 1.1

The Backward Design Approach Using the Capacities of the Literate Individual

Key Design Questions
Stage 1. What are the desired results?
(a) Which capacities of the literate individual does the unit address?
(b) What enduring understandings are desired?
(c) What key knowledge and skills will students acquire as a result of this unit?
Stage 2. What is the evidence of understanding?
(a) Through what performance-based task will students demonstrate achievement of the desired results?
(b) Through what other evidence will students demonstrate achievement of the desired results?
(c) How will students reflect upon and assess their literacy development?
Stage 3. What learning experiences and instruction will enable students to achieve the desired results?
(a) What learning experiences and teaching will promote student understanding, interest, and excellence?
(b) What sources will be used to promote student understanding, interest, and excellence?
(c) What teaching methods will be employed to promote understanding, interest, and excellence?

Source: Adapted from Wiggins & McTighe, 2005.

Backward design mirrors what test developers like PARCC and Smarter Balanced do. These organizations think about what students who are on the path to college and career readiness ought to be able to do (identify desired results, or outcomes), and they design measures to assess where students are in their development (determine acceptable evidence). Smarter Balanced (n.d.) explains this clearly:

> The Smarter Balanced assessment system will cover the full range of college- and career-ready knowledge and skills in the Common Core State Standards. To do this, each test item is associated with assessment targets and overall content claims. Content claims are major categories for looking at student performance. The assessment targets were developed to ensure item writers and reviewers address the standards, learning progressions, and the range of thinking possible. (para. 13)

The next generation of assessments is being developed based on clear standards and expectations known to all stakeholders:

> The critical nature of content alignment became clear to all educators as a result of the Debra P. vs. Turlington case in 1981, in which it was ruled that the content of a test must be aligned to curriculum/instruction to be fair. This is intended to be accomplished by being aligned to the same content standards, thereby assuring that students have had the opportunity to learn the tested material. (Smarter Balanced, 2012, p. 8)

In the current testing climate, some of the means of measuring learning outcomes may be out of teachers' hands, but the inputs are still up to us. If we keep the literacy competencies in mind as we design our instruction, we will guide students' skill development and content knowledge toward college and career readiness, ensuring their success on the assessments designed to measure just that.

2

How Has Testing Changed?

As we have stressed, this book is not about test preparation but about how to create rich and challenging lessons that will help middle and high school students develop essential and powerful literacy skills. So why talk about what's new with tests? Our purpose in this chapter is to pinpoint how next generation tests provide evidence of student learning, and then consider what other kinds of evidence teachers who are committed to developing these capabilities might want to gather. How does the evidence of literacy learning that *you* value compare or contrast with the evidence that today's tests generate?

Often, a teacher's first instinct is to say that tests are what is wrong with the education system. Tests measure the wrong things, or they give an unfair advantage to students who work well under pressure or within a particular format. With these thoughts in mind, we were a little surprised when our inquiry into the current crop of assessments turned up some decidedly positive attributes. As you look at the sample questions in this chapter and think about how these next generation assessments were constructed, we hope that you will pick up on the beneficial qualities that we did and begin to see these tests in a more constructive light.

What Has Testing Changed?

When evaluating what makes a "next generation" or "21st century" assessment different from assessments past, the first thing to consider is the format of the exam. The PARCC exam is designed to be taken electronically, and the Smarter Balanced exam can be taken either electronically or with pen and paper, although the latter option will be phased out by 2018. The ACT moved to an electronic version in 2015, and the SAT will be offered electronically by 2016, although students will still have the option of taking a pencil-and-paper version of both tests.

The move to electronic testing introduces new dimensions to the format of questions and prompts, which have expanded beyond multiple-choice or essay questions. Figure 2.1 outlines the types of questions found on the PARCC and Smarter Balanced exams. Note especially the technology-enhanced questions.

Although new test formats highlighted in Figure 2.1 relate directly to the sixth of the capacities of the literate individual,

FIGURE 2.1
PARCC and Smarter Balanced Question Types

PARCC	Smarter Balanced
Evidence-Based Selected-Response (EBSR) questions/prompts are paired multiple-choice questions. One part (usually, Part A) measures students' comprehension and higher-order thinking about the text. The other part (usually, Part B) requires students to provide textual evidence to support their thinking.	**Selected-response items** prompt students to select one or more responses from a set of options.
Technology-Enhanced Constructed-Response (TECR) questions/prompts are similar to the EBSR questions in terms of purpose—providing evidence to support an answer. With the TECR, students can highlight, drag, and drop text into an organizer.	**Technology-enhanced items** capitalize on technology to collect evidence through a nontraditional response type, such as editing text or drawing an object. Selected-response and technology-enhanced items can be scored automatically.
Prose Constructed-Response (PRC) is an essay. In grades 6–12, there are two kinds of PRCs—a *research simulation task* and a *literary analysis task*.	**Constructed-response items** are open-ended and prompt students to produce a text or numerical response in order to collect evidence about their knowledge or understanding of a given assessment target.
	Matching tables call for students to match information in varied categories. For example, students check off which items in the right column relate to a category in the left column. This is often used with research and listening items.
	Performance tasks are a simulation of a research task that involve a scenario, reading multiple sources, and answering three research questions (one machine-scored and the other two constructed-response) meant to familiarize students with the sources and encourage critical thinking. Students then utilize their notes from the sources that they've analyzed to develop a research-based, written product for the audience and purpose designated in the scenario.

Source: Column 1—PARCC, 2014; Column 2—Smarter Balanced, 2015a.

use technology strategically and capably, next generation testing incorporates the other CLI as well. All of these elements are important components of the new tests, but perhaps the most important are the requirements that students be able to read complex texts independently and be able to analyze and utilize evidence. In fact, we would argue that the other six capacities hinge on students' mastery of these two.

New tests like those from PARCC and Smarter Balanced give a sense of the values that are guiding assessment's new direction. In 2015, the College Board published an overview of the changes made to the SAT—basically, a comparison of the old version and the new one released in March 2016. We've amended a table from that article with a column comparing the construct of the redesigned SAT to the current ACT (see Figure 2.2).

FIGURE 2.2

A Comparison of the Old SAT, the Redesigned SAT, and the Current ACT

Features	Old SAT	Redesigned SAT	Current ACT
Time Allotted	3 hours and 45 minutes	3 hours (plus 50 minutes for the optional essay)	3 hours and 12 minutes (plus 30 minutes for the optional essay)
Components	1. Critical Reading 2. Writing 3. Mathematics 4. Essay	1. Evidence-based reading and writing • Reading test • Writing and Language test 2. Mathematics 3. Essay (optional)	1. English 2. Mathematics 3. Reading 4. Science 5. Essay (optional)
Essay	Required and given at the beginning of the SAT: • 25 minutes to write the essay • Tests writing skill; students take a position on a presented issue.	Optional and given at the end of the SAT. Postsecondary institutions determine whether they will require the essay for admission. • 50 minutes to write the essay • Tests reading, analysis, and writing skills; students produce a written analysis of a provided source text.	Optional • 30 minutes to write the essay • Measures writing skills emphasized in high school English classes and in entry-level college composition courses

Source: Adapted from College Board (2015a).

According to the College Board (2014d), there are five major changes to the SAT that relate to literacy. Figure 2.3 lists those changes, along with the CLI each represents. Let's look at each change individually and consider how it also shows up in elements of the ACT, PARCC, Smarter Balanced, and state tests.

FIGURE 2.3

Literacy-Related Changes to the SAT and the Corresponding Capacities of the Literate Individual

Revised SAT's Literacy-Related Changes	Capacities of the Literate Individual
Focus on [vocabulary] words in context	Demonstrate independence when reading complex text
Command of evidence	Value evidence
Essay analyzing a source	Respond to the varying demands of audience, task, purpose, and discipline Comprehend as well as critique
Analysis in science and in history/social studies	Build strong content knowledge Comprehend as well as critique Use technology and digital media strategically and capably
Founding documents and great global conversation	Build strong content knowledge Comprehend as well as critique Understand other perspectives and cultures

Vocabulary in Context

First, shifting the call for students to master sometimes obscure vocabulary words to the expectation that they be able to understand *vocabulary in context* encourages students' development of close reading skills and better reflects the skills developed in classes and used in life. How many adults do you see on the subway or in the park memorizing vocabulary with flashcards? But you *do* see many adults reading, and we can be sure that they are encountering unfamiliar or less familiar words and using context to make sense of what those words mean. Testing that focuses on vocabulary in context is really addressing a student's ability to *read complex text independently*.

Figure 2.4 shows sample items from PARCC, Smarter Balanced, the ACT, the SAT, and the Massachusetts state ELA exam that address vocabulary in context.

FIGURE 2.4

Items Focused on Vocabulary Words in Context

SAT	The word "striking" in line 58 most nearly means A. removing B. pounding C. thoughtful D. remarkable E. believable *Source:* Robinson & Katzman, 2014, p. 583.
ACT	As it is used in line 5, the word *stature* most nearly means A. height B. achievement C. power D. status *Source:* Roell, 2012, p. 154.
Smarter Balanced (Grade 8)	First, read the dictionary definition. Then, complete the task. (*n*) 1. caretaker Click on the word in the paragraphs that *most closely* matches the definition provided. Ansel soon had plenty of opportunities to practice his photography. Starting when he was eighteen, he spent four summers in Yosemite National Park as a custodian for the Sierra Club headquarters. He led hiking expeditions though Yosemite and captured spectacular photographs with each hike.

(continued)

FIGURE 2.4 (*continued*)

Items Focused on Vocabulary Words in Context

Smarter Balanced (Grade 8)	He created his photos carefully, as though they were paintings like those seen at the Expo. Early in the twentieth century, photography was not considered creative art, but Ansel hoped to change that. He'd seen how the use of light and shade in paintings could bring them to life, and he wanted to use his camera to paint with light. He visualized the story he wanted to tell with each photo. "The picture we make is never made for us alone," he said later. "It is, and should be, a communication—to reach as many people as possible." Photographs, he felt, could create the same strong feelings the paintings at the Expo had aroused in him. *Source:* Smarter Balanced, 2014a, Sample Item 2674.
PARCC (Grade 9)	Part A Which three terms does the author use to refer to the "DNA fingerprint" that help clarify the meaning of the term? A. "...genetic photograph..." B. "...science of genetics..." C. "...individual crop varieties..." D. "...radioactive probes..." E. "...pattern unique to the organism..." F. "...desirable new traits..." G. "...genetic blueprint..." Part B What do these terms indicate about the results of the seven-step procedure to develop a DNA fingerprint? A. The procedure identifies a constantly evolving arrangement of genes. B. The procedure identifies a generally accurate arrangement of genes. C. The procedure identifies an uncomplicated arrangement of genes. D. The procedure identifies a set arrangement of genes. *Source:* PARCC, 2013, Sample Item #1.
State Exam (Grade 8)	In paragraph 5, the quotation marks surrounding "recipe" mainly indicate A. a word used in dialogue. B. an opinion of the author. C. a term used by many historians. D. an uncommon meaning of the word. *Source:* Massachusetts Department of Secondary Education, 2013, p. 101.

Notice that the last three items in Figure 2.4 look fairly similar, with the context provided in the form of line or paragraph numbers. PARCC and Smarter Balanced require students to choose the context that best supports their answers. The Smarter Balanced sample question illustrates how electronic testing can alter the construction of multiple-choice questions. Here, instead of choosing the correct answer from a list of distractors (incorrect answers), students click on the evidence that supports their answer. In other Smarter Balanced test items, students respond by clicking on, dragging, or highlighting text. This type of technology-enhanced question can be found on the PARCC exam as well.

The PARCC example in Figure 2.4 represents a two-part question. It is an interesting construct for a vocabulary question, because rather than the typical setup (in Part A, students select the best definition; in Part B, they tell which textual evidence best supports that definition), two-part questions ask students to identify context clues in Part A and discuss the implication of the phrase in Part B. Students must answer both parts correctly in order to get full credit, although when a part has multiple answers (e.g., students can select from multiple context clues in Part B), it's possible to earn partial credit for a partially correct answer. We will discuss scoring further in the next section.

Command of Evidence

If we had to sum up the major change in testing in one word, that word would be *evidence*. Whereas on past exams, students could guess at answers and stand a chance of choosing the right one, now there is a stronger focus on students providing a rationale or evidence to support their answers. Figure 2.5 shows some sample items that measure students' command of evidence.

The SAT prompt requires students to analyze an author's use of evidence, reasoning, and style in a piece of writing. The ACT prompt requires students to answer questions based on specific evidence provided in the form of line numbers within the text

---

FIGURE 2.5
Items Focused on Command of Evidence

SAT	As you read the passage below, consider how Dana Gioia [the author] uses • Evidence, such as facts or examples to support claims. • Reasoning to develop ideas and to connect claims and evidence. • Stylistic or persuasive elements, such as word choice or appeals to emotion, to add power to the ideas expressed. *Source:* College Board, 2015c, Essay 2.
ACT	The information in lines 22–30 deals primarily with A. Evidence for the author's belief that Smith's version of his rescue might not be entirely accurate. B. An attempt to disprove the commonly held theory that Pocahontas and Smith were romantically involved. C. The kind of behavior that would have been expected from a Native American girl during the colonial era. D. The analysis of an incident at the colonial fort during which Pocahontas performed cartwheels. *Source:* Martz, Magloire, & Silver, 2014, p. 743.
Smarter Balanced (Grade 7)	Click on *all* the sentences from the excerpt below that support the idea that a high population of moose will lead to a decrease in their numbers. Scientists have been studying this isolated food chain for 50 years to understand how changes in one link can cause changes in another. As more moose are born on the island, they eat more balsam fir. The more they consume, the more they damage the trees. Stunted trees mean less food. Eventually, there's not enough food to support the moose. Many starve, and their numbers decrease. With fewer moose dining on them, the fir trees eventually recover. *Source:* Smarter Balanced, 2013, Sample Item 839.
PARCC (Grade 10)	Part A Which option *best* captures a central theme of the passage? a. the stimulation of the imagination b. the overcoming of childhood fears c. the disruption of nature by humans d. the deceptive nature of dreams Part B Which quotation is most relevant to the central theme of the passage? a. "They could still see each other's faces when they left the house, but by the time they reached the river it was only a short pitch of dark." (paragraph 1) b. "A river it was called; actually it was no more than a ditch through the paddies, a little wider perhaps than most ditches, with plumes of grass bending over it from either bank and almost closing off the surface. A bridge was still dimly visible . . . " (paragraph 1) c. "They turned off their flashlights and approached in silence; fireflies dislike noise and light." (paragraph 2) d. "Dark, dreamy, rather . . . might one say? Perhaps something of the child's world, the world of the fairy story in it. . . . Something not to be painted but to be set to music, the mood of it taken up on a piano or a koto." (paragraph 2) *Source:* PARCC, 2015b, p. 13.

FIGURE 2.5 (*continued*)
Items Focused on Command of Evidence

State Exam (Grades 9–11)	**Part A** Why does the author mention the horror movie *Jaws* and a nature show about sea creatures? • To show why the narrator is intimidated by the unknown • To show that snorkeling in the ocean can be dangerous • To reinforce the idea that the unknown can be challenging • To help describe what the narrator sees while snorkeling **Part B** Select the detail from the passage that supports the answer to Part A. • "I wasn't one of those people who refused to take a bath for a month after seeing the movie *Jaws*." • "Who knew what lay beneath it all? • "I had recently seen a nature show about the kinds of fish—if you could even call them fish—that inhabited the greatest depths of the oceans: grotesque, insect-like things with translucent bodies, huge eyes, and feelers that sprouted from their heads like some kind of alien appendages." • "I put on my mask and adjusted the snorkel along the side of my head as carefully as I could, knowing that I'd probably suck vast quantities of sea water through it just the same." *Source:* Tennessee Department of Education, 2015, p. 30.

passage. This prompt also focuses on literary devices (allusion, theme). Students must support their analysis of these literary devices with direct references to the text.

The PARCC sample in Figure 2.5 is another two-part EBSR item. According to PARCC, this particular question tests students' ability to meet Common Core Reading Standards 1 and 2 (grasping explicit meaning and inference; identifying central idea and supporting details/summary). Part B speaks to the prioritization of evidence throughout the PARCC exam. Students must choose evidence in Part B to support their chosen answer in Part A. If students choose the correct theme but do not choose appropriate evidence in Part B, they will receive 1 point. If they choose the wrong theme, they cannot earn any points. This type of question may involve multiple pieces of evidence in Part B. If there are multiple correct answers in Part B and a student only chooses one correct answer rather than the required number of answers, then that student may earn partial credit. Maureen likes to call this item's construction "multiple choice on steroids."

Smarter Balanced takes this emphasis on evidence even further. The sample Smarter Balanced question is a technology-enhanced item that requires students to "select the sentences that support the inference that the area is in danger of losing its moose population." This is very much like a multiple-choice question. However, the test maker provides no hints, and there are far more options to choose from (15 paragraphs!) than the four or five options that students might find in a traditional multiple-choice item.

Essay Analyzing a Source

In the revised SAT, the writing task has changed significantly, moving from an opinion piece to an essay in which students analyze the writing choices of an author. This is meant to be more representative of the kinds of writing that students do in college. Here's the College Board's explanation:

> The basic aim of the essay is to determine whether students can demonstrate college- and career-readiness proficiency in reading, writing, and analysis by comprehending a high-quality source text and producing a cogent and clearly written analysis of that text supported by critical reasoning and evidence drawn from the source. (College Board, 2014b, p. 1)

Take a look at the sample item set in Figure 2.6.

FIGURE 2.6
Items Focused on Analyzing a Source

SAT	As you read the passage below, consider how Paul Bogard [the author] uses • Evidence, such as facts or examples to support claims. • Reasoning to develop ideas and to connect claims and evidence. • Stylistic or persuasive elements, such as word choice or appeals to emotion, to add power to the ideas expressed. *Source:* College Board, 2015c, Essay 1.
ACT	Some high schools in the United States have considered spending a portion of their limited funding on a breakfast service for students. Some educators think that many students' performance is limited by poor nutrition and being hungry during the day. Other educators

FIGURE 2.6
Items Focused on Analyzing a Source

ACT	think that eating breakfast is a personal choice and the responsibility of students' families. In your opinion, should high schools spend some of their limited funding on a breakfast service for students?
	In your essay, take a position on this question. You may write about either of the two points of view given, or you may present a different point of view on this question. Use specific reasons and examples to support your position.
	Source: Dulan, 2012, p. 272.
Smarter Balanced (Grade 8)	A student is writing an editorial for the local newspaper about cell phones in schools. Read the draft of the editorial and complete the task that follows.
	Needing to Communicate
	Many parents want to be able to have access to their children via cell phones during the school day. However, with the regulations that are present at most schools, contacting their children can seem impossible to parents. While it is true that cell phones can be used improperly in a classroom, this problem can be avoided by establishing a clear set of rules. Instead of banning cell phones completely in schools, school districts should impose limits. These limits would help ensure that mobile devices are used for the right circumstances. For example, students would not be able to use phones during classes. They would, however, be able to use phones during breaks, such as lunch and after school. This limit would eliminate disruptive phone alerts during lessons but still enable appropriate use for students who are able to follow the rules and thus earn the privilege of carrying a phone.
	Write an introduction to the editorial that establishes and introduces a clear claim that supports the use of cell phones in schools.
	Source: Smarter Balanced, 2014a, Sample Item 2552.
PARCC (Grade 10)	You have read two passages, one from Jacey Choy's "Red Cranes" and one from Jun'ichiro Tanizaki's "The Firefly Hunt." Though Mie and Sachiko, the main characters in the passages, have certain similarities, the authors develop their characters in very different ways.
	Write an essay in which you analyze the different approaches the authors take to develop these characters. In your essay, be sure to discuss how each author makes use of such elements as
	• the main characters' intentions with other characters,
	• the presentation of the main characters' thoughts, and
	• the strong feelings each character experiences at the end of each passage.
	Use specific evidence from both passages to support your analysis.
	Source: PARCC, 2015b, Sample Item 7.
State Exam (English I)	After reading "Hearing the Sweetest Songs," do you think the author considers herself disabled? Explain your answer and support it with evidence from the selection.
	Source: Texas Education Agency, 2014, Short Answer #2.

The first thing you might notice is that the sample SAT item here is almost identical to the one in Figure 2.5. This is a reflection of how central an author's use of evidence is to this kind of textual analysis. Now notice that rather than asking for an analytical essay, the ACT writing task requires students to take a stance on a topic that is meant to be relevant to them and to develop an essay that represents their perspective on this issue. Although the essay does not include analysis of sources, it does require students to analyze their beliefs and the evidence that supports these beliefs, and to demonstrate an awareness of task, purpose, and audience in their writing. This is similar to the redesigned SAT writing task.

The state exam item shown, which is from the State of Texas Assessment of Academic Readiness (STARR), is similar to the ACT task in that students must take a stance on a topic (whether the author considers herself disabled). Note, however, the added element: the STARR task requires students to analyze and utilize text to support their answers. This is somewhat similar to the SAT task, which asks students to analyze the writing style of a work and explain how that style supports the author's intentions.

The Smarter Balanced Brief Write sample item in Figure 2.6 requires that students analyze the start of a piece of mock student writing. Then they are asked to either develop an introduction or conclusion working from mock notes, or develop further evidence to elaborate on the existing draft. In this example, students are analyzing a piece of writing that might be similar to something that they would produce. Other versions of this task might request them to analyze notes on a topic. The inclusion of the scenario in this task is unique to Smarter Balanced's approach. Given a scenario that makes clear the audience for and the purpose of the piece of writing, students must take this into account in the analysis and decision making that will drive their written response.

The prompt from the PARCC exam most closely matches that of the SAT because it is focused on analysis. Remember that in addition to the analysis task, PARCC includes a research simulation task for grades 6–12 (see Figure 2.7). Smarter Balanced also includes a performance task that requires students to simulate research (see Figure 2.8).

Like the SAT and PARCC literary analysis task, the PARCC research simulation task and the Smarter Balanced performance task focus students on close reading, a skill that is a strong identifier of college success. Unlike the literary analysis task, these tasks focus on analyzing informational text—traditional printed text but also multimedia sources, such as blogs and videos. They are a practical reflection of our information-rich age, where people regularly turn to TED Talks or YouTube for explanations of ideas and processes, and K–12 education is increasingly taking place well beyond classroom walls. More and more students are engaged in flipped classroom experiences, in which they are expected to view videos of instruction outside of a traditional school setting and be prepared to participate in meaningful conversation and activity based on that instruction during class time.

FIGURE 2.7
The PARCC Research Simulation Task

Overview	Sample Item (Grade 10)
Purpose: "… observation, deduction, and proper use and evaluation of evidence across text types." Construct of the task: • Learn about a topic by studying an anchor text. • Study more about the topic as presented in multiple sources (possibly including video). • Answer questions based on the sources. • Develop analytical essays based on the sources.	In 1968 three students in Des Moines, Iowa, arrived at their separate schools wearing black armbands to protest United States involvement in the Vietnam War. The principals of the schools quickly instituted a policy banning the wearing of armbands, leading to the suspension of the students. A lawsuit filed on behalf of the students was eventually argued in the Supreme Court on November 12, 1968. Today you will read two passages and listen to a short audio clip discussing the context and impact of the case. At the end of the task, you will be asked to write an analytical essay.

Sources: Column 1—PARCC, 2014, p. 11; Column 2—PARCC, 2015b, p. 19.

FIGURE 2.8

The Smarter Balanced Performance Task

Overview	Sample Item (Grade 11)
Purpose: • Integrate knowledge and skills • Measure understanding, research skills, analysis, and the ability to provide relevant evidence • Require students to plan, write, revise, and edit • Reflect a real-world task • Demonstrate knowledge and skills • Allow for multiple points of view • Be feasible for the classroom environment Task Construct: Students are presented with a scenario indicating purpose and audience for the research-based writing that they will develop. Students read multiple information texts related to a particular topic (including graphs, charts, and/or a simulated Internet search). Students respond to open-ended questions based on the sources. Students write an essay, report, or script based on the sources.	Your task In your economics class, you are discussing the importance of making smart financial decisions. Your teacher tells you that, in some school districts, students are required to take a financial literacy class before graduating. Your school board is hosting a meeting to decide whether to offer such a course for graduation, and wants students to contribute their perspectives. As part of your initial research, you have found four sources about financial literacy classes. After you have reviewed these sources, you will answer some questions about them. Briefly scan the sources and the three questions that follow. Then, go back and read the sources carefully so you will have the information you will need to answer the questions and finalize your research. You may click on the Global Notes button to take notes on the information you find in the sources as you read. You may also use scratch paper to take notes. In Part 2, you will write an argumentative essay on a topic related to the sources.

Sources: Column 1—Smarter Balanced, 2015b; Column 2— Smarter Balanced, 2014b.

The major difference between the PARCC research simulation task and the Smarter Balanced performance task is that the PARCC task asks students to analyze the arguments developed within sources and the Smarter Balanced task requires students to develop their own argument after analyzing sources. It is important to note that the Smarter Balanced items are scored by various contractors or vendors who use anchor papers that have been normed through a range-finding process that involved teachers and educators. Teachers also reviewed the Smarter Balanced performance tasks themselves and helped with the development of scoring rubrics.

Analysis in Science and in History/Social Studies

We see more evidence of the porousness of metaphorical classroom walls in the next generation tests' expectation that students will analyze science and history/social studies texts. The SAT, ACT, Smarter Balanced, and PARCC assessments all provide students with opportunities to apply literacy skills across varied writing *tasks* and varied informational *texts* (see Figure 2.9).

FIGURE 2.9

Items Focused on Text Analysis in Science and in History/Social Studies

SAT	[Read] the following passage . . . excerpted from a book by a naturalist who studied the behavior of coyotes living in Yellowstone Park. *Canis latrans* refers to the species of coyote she observed. The author mentions nineteenth-century explorers (lines 42–43) in order to A. denounce a traditional custom B. prove a controversial theory C. illustrate a scientific conundrum D. explain a temporary phenomenon E. provide evidence supporting a claim *Source:* Princeton Review, 2015, p. 628.
ACT	SOCIAL SCIENCE: [Read] this passage . . . adapted from *How to Develop Self-Esteem in Your Child: 6 Vital Ingredients* by Dr. Bettie Youngs. The author's purpose in writing this passage is to: A. Show that early childhood learning is important because it provides the foundation for life. B. Analyze the causes behind low self-esteem in children. C. Denounce child psychologists. D. Discuss the various behaviors associated with the ages of children. HUMANITIES: [Read] this passage . . . adapted from *A Guide to Early Printed Books and Manuscripts* by Mark Bland (Wiley). The author would argue that the primary difference between the quality of "being literary" and that of "thinking like a bibliographer" is: A. One requires an appreciation for literary texts, and the other ignores altogether the texts and their places in history. B. One considers the financial components of book making, and the other does not. C. One looks at the written page and sees a poem, and the other looks at a page and sees the relationship between type, paper, and space. D. One recognizes the relationship between form and meaning, and the other considers only the financial aspects of creating a literary work.

(continued)

FIGURE 2.9 (*continued*)

Items Focused on Text Analysis in Science and in History/Social Studies

ACT	NATURAL SCIENCE: [Read] this passage . . . adapted from *Reading the Weather* by T. Morris Lonstreth. According to the passage, what does the author consider dust's most important role? A. Serving as a heat collector B. Forming the basis of rain C. Minimizing the sun's glare D. Providing a thick layer of protection around the earth *Source:* Hatch & Hatch, 2015, p. 334.
Smarter Balanced (Grade 7)	Which of the following sentences from the passage best support this conclusion that all living organisms are part of the food chain? A. "The energy that you use to live every day travels from one living thing to another, in a chain that starts with the sun." B. "This energy then helps plants change water from the soil and carbon dioxide from the air into oxygen and carbohydrates that power their cells." C. "Food chains everywhere—in grasslands and deserts, oceans and tropical rainforests—begin with the producers." D. "Scientists have been studying this isolated food chain for 50 years to understand how changes in one link can cause changes in another." *Source:* Smarter Balanced, 2013, Item 838.
PARCC (Grade 8)	Today you will research an experiment involving elephants. First you will read an article about the experiment. Then you will view a video and read a passage of the actual study. As you review these sources, you will gather information and answer questions about how the sources present information so you can write an analytical essay. *Source:* PARCC, 2015a, p. 21.
State Exam (Grade 11)	Closely read each of the *four* texts provided on pages 11 through 17 and write a source-based argument on the topic below. You may use the margins to take notes as you read and scrap paper to plan your response. Write your argument beginning on page 1 of your essay booklet. Topic: Should extinct species be brought back into existence? Your Task: Carefully read each of the *four* texts provided. Then, using evidence from at least *three* of the texts, write a well-developed argument regarding whether extinct species should be brought back into existence. Clearly establish your claim, distinguish your claim from alternate or opposing claims, and use specific, relevant, and sufficient evidence from at least *three* of the texts to develop your argument. Do not simply summarize each text. *Source:* University of the State of New York, 2015, p. 2.

All five of these test items require students to think about science- or social studies–related topics after gathering information from one or more sources. It's a reflection of the tests' common and explicit commitment to these subject areas. The College Board claims that the work of the redesigned SAT will "engage teachers in science and history/social studies disciplines and reflect the work students are doing in those classrooms" (2014a, p. 1). The ACT includes a section on science that "assumes that students are in the process of taking the core science course of study (three years or more) that will prepare them for college-level work and have completed a course in earth science and/or physical science and a course in biology" (ACT, 2014b, para. 4). PARCC notes roughly a third of the items used to assess students' ability to comprehend and draw evidence from complex texts will incorporate science texts, and another third will incorporate social studies texts (PARCC, 2014, p. 17). Smarter Balanced states, "[Fifty-five percent] of text-related assessment evidence will come from reading informational texts and may include biographies, science, social studies, and technical texts/topics" (2011, p. 18).

Founding Documents and Great Global Conversation

On top of the next generation tests' mindful selection of informational and literary passages, we also see a move in the SAT and PARCC exams toward including historical documents (e.g., the U.S. Constitution, the Bill of Rights, and original letters and speeches written by historical figures) and readings that relate to global issues such as environmentalism, free trade, and human rights (see Figure 2.10).

The College Board provides a strong rationale for the decision to include these types of readings:

> Every time students take the redesigned SAT, they will encounter a passage from one of the founding documents or from a text from the global conversation. In this way, we hope that the redesigned SAT will inspire a close reading of these rich, meaningful, often profound texts,

FIGURE 2.10

Items Focused on Founding Documents and Great Global Conversation

SAT	[Read] the following passage … about the art and recreation of Southeastern Indians. The author mentions the loss of many of the Indians' artistic and architectural creations (lines 19–20) in order to A. criticize Indians' choice of materials. B. provide an explanation for a problem. C. underscore De Soto's appreciation for Indian creations. D. delineate an impressive course of events. E. anticipate a possible objection to a theory. *Source:* Robinson & Katzman, 2014, p. 580.
PARCC **(Grade 11)**	Today you will read two documents that were written at the time of the American Revolution and read a transcript of a video that gives further information about one of these documents. As you study these sources, pay particular attention to the rhetorical features of each source and the audience to which each one was addressed. At the end of the task, you will be asked to write an analytical essay. *Source:* PARCC, 2015c, p. 18.
State Exam **(Grade 9)**	The author includes quotations from Lewis and Clark's journals most likely to show 1 the historic language the explorers used. 2 his familiarity with the sites described in the journals. 3 the difference between unexplored and modern landscapes. 4 similarities between his impressions and those of the explorers. *Source:* Florida Department of Education, n.d., Item 17.

not only as a way to develop valuable college and career readiness skills but also as an opportunity to reflect on and deeply engage with issues and concerns central to informed citizenship. (College Board, 2015b, para. 19)

How Do These Changes Reflect the Picture of the Literate Individual?

Often, as educators, we are frustrated by the amount of "change" that is thrown at us. Yes, the use of quotes there reflects our belief that a lot of educational change is old wine in new bottles. In some ways, this is also true of the new assessments. There are general concepts and competencies—comprehension, vocabulary, writing, and so on—that have been tested in the past, and those continue to be tested. However, the next generation assessments do feature important changes to note. Figure 2.11 lists those key changes, provides a sample assessment task that represents each change, and indicates the capacities of the literate individual that are measured by the sample tasks shown. This figure is our attempt to make explicit how the new assessments are striving to provide a better measure of students' development as literate individuals.

Consistent throughout all of these changes is the focus on complex texts. According to PARCC,

> the Common Core State Standards describe reading instruction as a shared responsibility within the school. . . . The grades 6–12 standards are divided into two sections: Standards for English Language Arts and Literacy Standards for History/Social Studies, Science, and Technical Subjects. This division reflects the unique, time-honored place of ELA teachers in developing students' literacy skills while at the same time recognizing that teachers in other areas must have a role in this development. Consequently, the PARCC assessments will be a reflection of the student achievement in literacy based on comprehending a range of sufficiently complex texts from a variety of genres and disciplines. (PARCC, 2014, p. 3)

Perhaps rather than speak of "changes," we should use the word *enhancements*. What we see in these next generation tests are enhanced ways of measuring core skills and knowledge. With technological advancements in testing and a strong focus on identifying outcomes that indicate the likelihood of success in college and career, testing really is being enhanced. This leads us to the big question facing educators: "How do I create lessons that will help my students achieve next generation literacy?" Of course we want students to be successful on the tests they are required to take. But we're teachers. What's most important for us is that our students be well educated, that

FIGURE 2.11

Connecting Test Changes and the Capacities of the Literate Individual

Test Change	Sample Assessment Item	Corresponding CLI
1. Focus on vocabulary in context	Smarter Balanced (Grade 8) First, read the dictionary definition. Then, complete the task. (*n*) 1. caretaker Click on the word in the paragraphs that *most closely* matches the definition provided. Ansel soon had plenty of opportunities to practice his photography. Starting when he was eighteen, he spent four summers in Yosemite National Park as a custodian for the Sierra Club headquarters. He led hiking expeditions though Yosemite and captured spectacular photographs with each hike. He created his photos carefully, as though they were paintings like those seen at the Expo. Early in the twentieth century, photography was not considered creative art, but Ansel hoped to change that. He'd seen how the use of light and shade in paintings could bring them to life, and he wanted to use his camera to paint with light. He visualized the story he wanted to tell with each photo. "The picture we make is never made for us alone," he said later. "It is, and should be, a communication—to reach as many people as possible." Photographs, he felt, could create the same strong feelings the paintings at the Expo had aroused in him. *Source:* Smarter Balanced, 2014a, Sample Item 2674.	Demonstrate independence reading complex text
2. Command of evidence	ACT The Information in lines 22–30 deals primarily with: A. evidence for the author's belief that Smith's version of his rescue might not be entirely accurate. B. an attempt to disprove the commonly held theory that Pocahontas and Smith were romantically involved. C. the kind of behavior that would have been expected from a Native American girl during the colonial era. D. the analysis of an incident at the colonial fort during which Pocahontas performed cartwheels. *Source:* Martz et al., 2014, p. 743.	Value evidence

FIGURE 2.11 (*continued*)

Connecting Test Changes and the Capacities of the Literate Individual

Test Change	Sample Assessment Item	Corresponding CLI
3. Essay analyzing a source	Sample PARCC Research Simulation Task (Grade 7) In 1968 three students in Des Moines, Iowa, arrived at their separate schools wearing black armbands to protest United States involvement in the Vietnam War. The principals of the schools quickly instituted a policy banning the wearing of armbands, leading to the suspension of the students. A lawsuit filed on behalf of the students was eventually argued in the Supreme Court on November 12, 1968. Today you want to read two passages and listen to a short audio clip discussing the context and impact of the case. At the end of the task, you will be asked to write an analytical essay. *Source:* PARCC, 2015b, p. 19.	Respond to the varying demands of audience, task, purpose, and discipline Comprehend as well as critique
4. Analysis in science and in history/social studies	PARCC (Grade 8) Today you will research an experiment involving elephants. First, you will read an article about the experiment. Then you will view a video and read a passage of the actual study. As you review these sources, you will gather information and answer questions about how the sources present information so you can write an analytical essay. *Source:* PARCC, 2015a, p. 21.	Build strong content knowledge Comprehend as well as critique Use technology and digital media strategically and capably
5. Founding documents and great global conversation	SAT [Read] the following passage . . . about the art and recreation of Southeastern Indians. The author mentions the loss of many of the Indians' artistic and architectural creations (lines 19–20) in order to A. criticize Indians' choice of materials. B. provide an explanation for a problem. C. underscore De Soto's appreciation for Indian creations. D. delineate an impressive course of events. E. anticipate a possible objection to a theory. *Source:* Robinson & Katzman, 2014, p. 580.	Comprehend as well as critique Understand other perspectives and cultures

they be prepared for college and career, and that they develop the capacities of the literate individual, which will serve them throughout their lives.

The teacher's role in supporting students' literacy development is the focus of the second part of this book.

PART II

In the Classroom
Developing the Capacities
of the Literate Individual

In this part of the book, we explore ways to help students develop the capacities of the literate individual (CLI). The next six chapters address six of the seven capacities—all of them save independence with complex text, a capacity that emerges from the development of the other six.

Each chapter focuses on a specific CLI and follows a standard pattern designed to model the process of creating test-informed ELA lessons to build next generation literacy:

1. We deconstruct the CLI by highlighting two or three descriptors that isolate its component skills. In other words, we look closely at what students must be able to do in order to *build strong content knowledge, comprehend as well as critique, value evidence,* and so on.

2. We share a sample assessment item from or directly modeled on a state test or the SAT, ACT, PARCC, or Smarter Balanced exams and tease out the connections between the assessment task and the component skills of the CLI.

3. We describe a lesson designed to help students build the CLI's component skills, focusing on effective instructional

strategies and highlighting how each of these strategies can be deployed to support differentiation and help learners with varied needs engage with lesson content and build literacy.

If this three-part construct sounds familiar, it should! It is backward design. The targeted CLI is *Stage 1: Desired Result*, the test item functions as *Stage 2: Evidence*, and the lesson represents *Stage 3: Instructional Procedures*. Maybe you remember the prompts in Figure 1.1, but in case you do not (and to save you from flipping back), here's a reminder of the key questions that we need to ask ourselves for these stages:

• Stage 1: What are the desired results?
• Stage 2: What is the evidence of understanding?
• Stage 3: What learning experiences and instruction will enable students to achieve the desired results?

The CLI and test questions help us know where we're headed, but it is up to us to decide how best to get there. For each CLI, we ask ourselves, "What engaging means can we use to develop students' knowledge and understanding?"

Over Part II's chapters and sample lessons, we share 42 instructional strategies for developing next generation literacy. Although these strategies are presented in connection with a particular capacity, there is a lot of functional overlap; several strategies are effective in fostering more than one CLI. (See the Conclusion for an overview of which strategies can be effectively used to promote which CLI.) In short, we present these teaching strategies as a set of tools that you and your students can use to develop knowledge and skills.

Please note that each of the lesson examples in Part II has a strong focus on differentiation. In education classes, the term *differentiation* is tossed around like a Hacky Sack on the quad. Students and teachers alike know the importance of being able to differentiate content, process, and product. For example, in the sample lesson in Chapter 3, which involves creating an environmental campaign (see pp. 46–47), differentiation of content and process is evident in the choice of topic students have within the frame of environmentalism and the varied sources they're asked to consult (written texts, online texts, video of spoken presentations, classmates during discussion). Differentiation of product comes from the various ways students are asked to demonstrate their learning: through speaking in a debate or evaluating the debaters, by writing a formal piece of argumentation (a proposal), or by developing a more creative persuasive piece (a flyer).

In each CLI-focused chapter, we include reflection questions for all three stages of backward design. If you are currently in the classroom, you can use these questions to capitalize on what is going well and to shine a light on areas where you want to grow. If you are a preservice teacher, you might apply these questions to classroom observations or use them as a basis for reflecting on your own K–12 experiences.

Finally, we want to stress that the sample lesson scenarios we provide are just that—*samples*. Each is a demonstration of how strategies may be combined in a particular learning experience, but they are not meant to dictate how to teach *your* students. You may want to address more than one capacity in a lesson or combine strategies presented in different lessons. Our greatest intent is to remind you that teaching doesn't have to be about teaching to the test, and that creative, meaningful teaching and learning lead naturally to students' success on exams and, more important, success in life.

3

Building Strong Content Knowledge

Students establish a base of knowledge across a wide range of subject matter by engaging with works of quality and substance. They become proficient in new areas through research and study. They read purposefully and listen attentively to gain both general knowledge and discipline-specific expertise. They refine and share their knowledge through writing and speaking. (CCSSI, 2015)

Living in our society today means being bombarded with information—from newspapers, magazines, television, radio, the Internet, and more. A 2007 study by the University of California revealed that when all of these sources were considered, along with Twitter, Facebook, and e-mail, the average person received 174 newspapers' worth of information each day. That's stunning in itself, but consider that the researchers compared their findings with the average intake of information in 1986, which was the equivalent of 40 newspapers (Alleyne, 2011). We'll do the math for you. Over a 24-year period, people's information intake increased by 230 percent. It's safe to say that the amount of information coming at us—and at our students—will only continue to increase.

This makes a good case for why students must learn to distinguish information of quality and substance when they go about assembling an understanding of the world around them. There is cause for concern that our students are falling short when it comes to the reading and listening skills they need to build content knowledge. According to a 2014 report, for example, only 26 percent of students who took the ACT in 2013 met the benchmark for college and career readiness in reading (ACT, 2014a).

In this chapter, we explore methods and strategies that support students' ability to build strong content knowledge—a key capacity of next generation literacy. Remember, the description of the literate individual captures where we want students to be by the time they graduate. What can we do to ensure that more of our students are developing this critical CLI? The three stages of the backward design model (Desired Results, Evidence, and Instructional Procedures) provide a structure for our planning.

Stage 1: Desired Results

In the description of this CLI, we find three key components. To *build strong content knowledge*, students must be able to

1. Read purposefully.
2. Listen attentively.
3. Share through writing and speaking.

Stage 1 Reflection

Are you deliberately pursuing these outcomes in your instruction now? Pick out a few lessons that have these skills among the objectives and reflect on the methods and strategies that you are using to promote students' development of these skills. Are there other skills you see as essential to building strong content knowledge?

Stage 2: Evidence

To get a sense of how today's test makers are assessing students' ability to build content knowledge, let's take a look at a sample research simulation task from PARCC.

SAMPLE TEST ITEM
PARCC Research Simulation Task, Grade 8

Today you will research an experiment involving elephants. First you will read an article about an experiment. Then you will view a video and read a passage from the actual study of the experiment. As you review these sources, you will gather information and answer questions about how the sources present information so that you can write an analytical essay.

Source: PARCC, 2015a.

Our own analysis begins by looking closely at the demands of the test—by breaking the task into its components and clarifying how each relates to building strong content knowledge:

Demands of the Test	CLI Skill Components
Students read the article and the passage from the study.	Read purposefully.
Students listen while viewing the video of the study.	Listen attentively.
Students write an analytical essay.	Share through writing and speaking.

This task closely parallels the kind of research students are doing in today's classrooms. They aren't just reading printed texts; they're also viewing videos and utilizing the Internet to access a variety of sources. Note that while this sample question from PARCC calls for students to demonstrate their content knowledge by writing an analytical essay, a parallel task on the Smarter Balanced exam might call for students to give an oral presentation regarding the information gathered from the sources.

Stage 2 Reflection

Is this assessment approach one that you use in your classroom? How do you gauge the progress students are making in their ability to build content knowledge? How do you ask them to reflect upon and assess their own learning?

Stage 3: Instructional Procedures

In our experience, the key to building content knowledge is engagement—having a compelling purpose for learning and the drive to pursue it. We doubt that anyone reading this book favors leading students to believe that the purpose of school is to earn a good grade or pass tests. Fortunately, it's possible to infuse a natural sense of purpose into lessons by connecting classroom content and skills with students' interests and with real-world applications. The sample lesson we're about to share does this through service learning.

According to Guilfoile and Ryan (2013), "Service-learning is one of several 'deeper learning' strategies that states, districts, schools, and teachers may use to help students gain a deeper understanding of core academic content and simultaneously build deeper learning skills through the integration of content knowledge with application (p. 3)."

In our experience, when students are completing a task simply to earn a grade, they may be operating in a way that is mechanical. By contrast, when students believe that their work can bring about change, they tend to be more focused readers and more committed learners.

Here is a sample lesson scenario that incorporates service learning and provides a frame for talking more specifically about the instructional techniques that can support the development of content knowledge.

SAMPLE LESSON SCENARIO
Developing a Campaign

Maureen's class began discussing environmentalism. The students had read some passages from Rachel Carson's *Silent Spring* and were considering what their modern version of this text, addressing concerns important to them, might look like. The class came to an agreement to focus on how eating meat affects the environment and personal health. This was a student-directed decision. Although there were some vegetarians in the class, there were even more students who were interested in changing the school lunch menu!

SAMPLE LESSON SCENARIO (*continued*)
Developing a Campaign

As research, Maureen's students read articles and explored websites related to vegetarianism and the environment. They viewed TED Talks by Mark Bittman, a food writer for the *New York Times,* and Ann Cooper, the chef who revolutionized school cafeterias by making healthier food choices available to students. Based on their findings, the students staged a debate about how far society has come since Rachel Carson wrote *Silent Spring*, developed formal written proposals to the school administration regarding the implementation of a Meatless Monday Campaign to convince students to give up meat one day a week, and designed informational flyers to convince their peers to take part in this movement.

Connecting the Lesson with the CLI

Let's begin by considering what this lesson looks like through the lens of the target CLI—*build strong content knowledge*:

CLI Skill Components	Lesson Components
Read purposefully.	Students read articles and explore websites related to topics that interest them: vegetarianism and environmentalism.
Listen attentively.	Students listen to TED Talk presentations related to the content.
Share through writing and speaking.	Students participate in a debate (speaking) and express opinions formed through research.
	Students develop a formal proposal for the administration (writing), making a case built on research.
	Students develop a flyer for their peers (writing), making a case built on research.

Guiding Students' Development: Skills and Strategies

Next, let's look at ways to support the development of the literacy capacity this lesson targets by focusing on the CLI's component skills and some instructional strategies to help build those skills.

Read purposefully

The first way to help students develop as purposeful readers is simply to help them see a purpose for their reading. In this case, Maureen let student interest serve as the purpose driver, allowing the class to choose a research topic related to the text. They connected the idea of environmentalism with their desire to see change in the cafeteria food offerings.

Interest is a powerful driver. A great way to extend efforts to connect to student interests beyond the "Tell us about yourself" inventories we tend to distribute at the beginning of the school year is to ask students what they would like to change about their school, their town, their country, their world. Encourage them to see themselves as positive forces rather than passive bystanders. Stress that they can bring about change if they find the right tools and the right support.

Even when students choose a topic of study that they care about, they may still need guidance to help them read purposefully. Here are some strategies to try.

Directed Reading Thinking Activity (DRTA)

Directed Reading Thinking Activity (DRTA) is a strategy for guiding comprehension of a reading selection. DRTAs vary in format from source to source, but the following components are present in all plans:

• *Pre-reading:* Draw or build upon background knowledge of the topic.

• *Skill development:* Predict what the reading will be about by scanning the title, headings, illustrations, and other indicators.

—Review or introduce new vocabulary.

—Review how to pay attention to boldfaced words.

—Review effective use of context clues.

• *During reading:* Guide the reading.

— Distribute prepared print or digital copies of the reading, and have students read silently to stopping points, at which time they will pause and answer questions listed in the margin.

— Have students pay attention to bolded vocabulary words.

— Choose some students to read aloud and discuss the parts related to the questions.

• *Post reading:* Assign follow-up activities, such as developing additional questions related to the reading, interviewing a peer or adult about his or her knowledge of the topic, or finding and reading a related work.

Differentiation highlights/tips: DRTA is an effective strategy for all learners. English language learners (ELLs) benefit from the scaffolding provided by reviewing terminology before reading. Struggling readers benefit from the review of reading strategies, such as paying attention to bolded information and utilizing context clues. The questions during the reading help students stay focused. You can vary the questions to match your students' ability levels or ask students to generate their own questions at the identified stopping points. You can also vary the setup of this activity to accommodate students' learning styles, with independent learners working alone and those with a more interpersonal learning style reading and answering the questions in pairs.

Double-Sided Notes

This strategy requires students to assemble evidence to support their thinking. There are many options for using double-sided notes; Figure 3.1 shows a general structure that works with a variety of sources.

FIGURE 3.1
Double-Sided Notes Structure

I think that . . .	I think this because the text says . . .

Differentiation highlights/tips: The Double-Sided Notes strategy is effective for ELLs and struggling readers because it reminds them to read closely for evidence to support their thinking. You can scaffold this strategy by providing sentence starters within each column or extend it by adding another column with a heading like this: "This connects with something else that I've read because. . . ."

Annotation

All of us have our own methods of annotating text. As your students work to find an approach that works for them, we recommend providing a modified version of the Great Books method as an instructive model:

* = Something important
! = Strong reaction
? = Question

Begin using these symbols in read-aloud situations and text assignments. To support formative assessment, we recommend asking students to make an actual note (a few words or sentence) in the text margin next to each of their symbols. This will make their thinking more overt when they—and you—review their annotations.

Differentiation highlights/tips: Annotation is a skill that experienced readers take for granted, but it doesn't always come naturally. Middle and high school students still need support in learning what components of a text to annotate. The three simple categories—something important, strong reaction, and question—are good, straightforward forms of annotation that all learners should practice using. You can ask ELLs or struggling readers to circle words that they do not understand, and you can extend students' annotations by adding more symbols/categories such as T-S (text-to-self connection), T-T (text-to-text connection), or T-W (text-to-world connection) or by challenging students to develop and explain annotation symbols of their own.

Listen attentively

Passive listening is a temptation that's familiar to anyone who has ever sat in a classroom, lecture hall, or faculty meeting. The temptation is even greater when the presenter isn't actually in the room (as in a TED Talk or a flipped classroom) or when a projector goes on and the lights go out. Here are some strategies to support students' development as attentive listeners.

Guided Notes

When the lesson calls for students to follow spoken presentations or get information from a video, we recommend providing them with a set of questions or prompts to keep them focused. You may want to give everyone the same questions or prompts, or you may choose to have several small groups focusing on separate questions, which will generate multiple perspectives on the source.

Four Square

The Four Square graphic organizer builds on the idea of Guided Notes and prompts students to focus on four specific areas (see Figure 3.2). There will be times when you'll want to tailor your

FIGURE 3.2
Four Square Organizer

Big Ideas	Questions
Connections	Other

square categories for specific content, but the general Four Square organizer in the figure is appropriate for a variety of topics and in a variety of contexts.

Differentiation highlights/tips: Both Guided Notes and Four Square are strategies that help students stay focused throughout a listening (or a reading) activity. You are the one who will provide the guidance and the square categories, so there is a lot of flexibility for differentiation. Tailor these resources to suit the needs of your students by using multiple versions with different questions or categories. As you develop questions and prompts, also consider how well they cover the range of thinking in Bloom's taxonomy.

Reflective Listening

In this student-led strategy for discussion, every time a student offers an idea, other group members restate the speaker's point to confirm their understanding and check for faulty thinking before they add their own idea. Reflective Listening keeps group members engaged and encourages clear articulation of the connections between evidence and inferences.

Differentiation highlights/tips: Reflective Listening is especially beneficial for ELLs because it exposes them to multiple ways of stating information and provides opportunity for classmates to offer clarifying information.

Share through writing and speaking

It is important to offer students varied ways to share through writing and speaking. The next generation of communication continues to involve writing, and it certainly involves visual communication through video and images as well as oral communication in person or via web platforms. In the lesson scenario, students share a formal proposal for the school to adopt Meatless Mondays and work together to create an informational flyer to convince their peers to take part in this movement. Here are a few strategies to give students practice sharing their developing content knowledge with classmates.

Debate

Although many students get excited about the prospect of a classroom debate, some may not be comfortable speaking in front of others. Figures 3.3 and 3.4 represent ways to structure the class and assess both those who debate and those who listen attentively and critically to the debaters. On debate day, teams of three to five students represent each side of the issue. Each team makes an opening statement. Then the teacher moderates to ensure that the teams take turns presenting evidence to support their claims and refuting their opponents' claims. This volley continues until each side has presented sufficient evidence to support their view.

FIGURE 3.3
Debate Preparation Organizer

DEBATE PREPARATION

Tomorrow, you will be taking part in a class debate. All students must be prepared to debate BOTH sides of the topics discussed below. Use the following organizer to prepare.

Resolved: We are at war with nature. In paragraph 16, Carson claims that humankind is engaged in a "war against nature" and describes the targets of that war. Do you agree that targeting certain things for destruction (or at least control) means that we are at war with nature? Can we be at war with something that is not our intended target?

Yes. We are in a war with nature because we are trying to control it. *List THREE reasons to support this opinion.*

1.

2.

3.

No. We are not in a war with nature. *List THREE reasons to support this opinion.*

1.

2.

3.

FIGURE 3.4

Debate Day Organizer and Reflection Tool

DEBATE DAY!

During the debate, please listen for and record the following:

A. **One idea that contradicts what you believe about this topic.** How does that idea provide a powerful counter-argument to your beliefs?

B. **Two ideas that your classmates share that relate to points you listed on your DEBATE PREPARATION form.**

1. _____ shared the same idea that I had regarding _____.
That idea is . . .

2. _____ shared the same idea that I had regarding _____.
That idea is . . . . . .

C. **Follow-up:** What was the best argument that you heard today? Explain.

Note that we advise asking all students, even those who are not going to engage in the debate, to complete a Debate Preparation Organizer. (The one in Figure 3.3 is set up to reflect the debate in this chapter's lesson scenario.) The practice helps ensure that everyone has analyzed the issue from both perspectives and has synthesized new content knowledge. In our experience, students tend to be more critical of their own beliefs and develop a more refined sense of these beliefs when they are challenged to articulate a case for the side that they do *not* personally support.

Differentiation highlights/tips: Advance preparation for the debate allows students to think about what they are going to say before they speak in front of others. This is important for all learners, but it is especially important for ELLs, who may lack the confidence to express themselves verbally in their new language. The Debate Day Organizer and Reflection Tool helps all students stay engaged during the debate, whether or not they are comfortable speaking in front of the class.

Writing a Proposal

The formal voice of a proposal is a distinctive one. The commonality between a proposal and a persuasive flyer, the two ways that students express content knowledge via writing in this sample lesson, is that both require the assembly of impactful data that will convince a reader to agree with a stance or request. Discuss with students the most important elements to include in their proposal. A sample can help them decide how to structure their writing. (One that we recommend can be found at http://special children.about.com/od/familyissues/a/flextimememo.htm.)

Developing a Flyer

When students develop a research-based flyer, it is best to have them look at strong samples. We recommend having them examine a flyer or advertisement by an advocacy group and analyze its key components. Students will likely note a striking visual image, startling statistics, and a powerful quote. Prompts can help guide them toward other marks of effective messaging: What else do they see? Thinking back on the information they've acquired through their research and the understanding they've refined through their debate, which points do they think will resonate most with their intended audience (other kids at school)? This strategy gives students a chance to present the results of their research creatively and reminds them to keep evidence at the forefront of their thinking.

Differentiation highlights/tips: Providing samples of both a proposal and a flyer is beneficial for ELLs and struggling writers as it gives them a visual model for their work.

Making the Test Connection

Let's think back now to the PARCC research simulation task we reviewed earlier in the chapter (see p. 45). Figure 3.5 outlines

FIGURE 3.5

Building Strong Content Knowledge: Skill Components, Demands of the Test, and Classroom Strategies

CLI Skill Components	Demands of the Test	Classroom Strategies
Read purposefully.	Students read the article and the passage from the study.	DRTA Double-Sided Notes Annotation
Listen attentively.	Students listen while viewing the video of the study.	Guided Notes Four Square Reflective Listening
Share through writing and speaking.	Students write an analytical essay.	Debate Writing a Proposal Developing a Flyer

the CLI skill components that test question assesses, the construct it uses to measure each skill component, and the teaching strategies we recommend to prepare students to gain competency with each component.

Stage 3 Reflection

What activities, instruction, sources, and methods would promote your students' understanding, interest, and excellence in this literacy capacity? How do the lessons you use now and the strategies you currently employ to help your students build strong content knowledge parallel the instructional procedures presented in this chapter? What changes might you make?

The differentiated tangible products that the students created in this chapter's sample lesson, such as the proposal directed to the administration and the persuasive flyer designed creatively to attract their peers, connect with the CLI that we will discuss in the next chapter: Literate individuals *respond to varying demands of audience, task, purpose, and discipline.*

4

Responding to Audience, Task, Purpose, and Discipline

Students adapt their communication in relation to audience, task, purpose, and discipline. They set and adjust purpose for reading, writing, speaking, listening, and language use as warranted by the task. They appreciate nuances, such as how the composition of an audience should affect tone when speaking and how the connotations of words affect meaning. They also know that different disciplines call for different types of evidence (e.g., documentary evidence in history, experimental evidence in science). (CCSSI, 2015)

The ability to communicate appropriately relative to audience, task, purpose, and discipline is a capacity that's sorely needed. In the 2011 National Assessment of Educational Progress, just 24 percent of U.S. 8th graders and 12th graders performed at the proficient level in writing. Only 3 percent performed at the advanced level. All others in these cohorts demonstrated writing that was either basic or below basic (National Center for Educational Statistics, 2012).

Why do we see such lackluster performance from a generation that is constantly communicating via phone, e-mail, text message, and various online platforms? One reason could be that state standards and high-stakes testing are "shifting attention away from a broad program of writing instruction toward a much narrower focus on how best to answer particular types of test questions" (Applebee & Langer, 2009, p. 26). Following this hypothesis, we might improve our students' writing by stressing it as a key communication skill that is essential both inside and outside the classroom. As Kerr and Picciotti (1992) point out,

> Writing can serve as a means for exploring academic subject matter as well as students' own perceptions of understanding. At the same time, writing can serve another purpose: it can provide students with a means for examining discourse itself, enabling them to gain a greater awareness of—and thus control over—various discourse conventions." (p. 105)

Kerr and Picciotti's view of writing can be applied to oral communication as well. Students might improve their ability to communicate by exploring subject matter through discourse, considering their own perspectives on information, and analyzing how others communicate.

In this chapter, we explore methods and strategies for developing our middle and high school students' ability to tailor their written and spoken communication in response to the varying demands of audience, task, purpose, and discipline. Again, the framework of backward design (Desired Results, Evidence, and Instructional Procedures) provides a structure for our planning process.

Stage 1: Desired Results

This CLI contains two key descriptors. To *respond to varying demands of audience, task, purpose, and discipline*, students must be able to

1. Recognize how tone and connotation affect meaning.
2. Utilize discipline-specific types of evidence.

Stage 1 Reflection

Are you deliberately pursuing these outcomes in your instruction now? Pick out a few lessons that have these skills among the objectives and reflect on the methods and strategies that you are using to promote students' development of these skills. Are there other skills you see as essential to responding to audience, task, purpose, and discipline?

Stage 2: Evidence

To convey how today's test makers are opting to assess students' ability to communicate with audience, task, purpose, and discipline in mind, we will look at an ACT writing prompt.

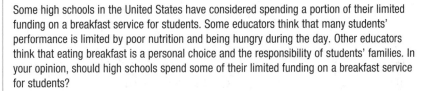

SAMPLE TEST ITEM
ACT Writing Prompt

Some high schools in the United States have considered spending a portion of their limited funding on a breakfast service for students. Some educators think that many students' performance is limited by poor nutrition and being hungry during the day. Other educators think that eating breakfast is a personal choice and the responsibility of students' families. In your opinion, should high schools spend some of their limited funding on a breakfast service for students?

In your essay, take a position on this question. You may write about either one of the two points of view given, or you may present a different point of view on this question. Use specific reasons and examples to support your position.

Source: Dulan, 2012, p. 272.

The top score that students can earn on this essay is a 6. According to the ACT, "Essays within this score range demonstrate effective skill in responding to the task." Here is the elaboration on what *effective skill* looks like:

> The essay shows a clear understanding of the task. The essay takes a position on the issue and may offer a critical context for discussion. The essay addresses complexity by examining different perspectives on the issue, or by evaluating the implications and/or complications of the issue, or by fully responding to counterarguments to the writer's position. Development of ideas is ample, specific, and logical. Most ideas are fully elaborated. A clear focus on the specific issue in the prompt is maintained. The organization of the essay is clear: the organization may be somewhat predictable or it may grow from the writer's purpose. Ideas are logically sequenced. Most transitions reflect the writer's logic and are usually integrated into the essay. The introduction and conclusion are effective, clear, and well developed. The essay shows a good command of language. Sentences are varied and word choice is varied and precise. There are few, if any, errors to distract the reader. (ACT, 2015, para. 10)

Let's clarify how the components of this writing prompt relates to our targeted CLI: *Respond to varying demands of audience, task, purpose, and discipline:*

Demands of the Test	CLI Skill Components
Students will show "a good command of language. Sentences are varied and word choice is varied and precise."	Recognize how tone and connotation affect meaning.
Students will use varied evidence based on the prompt.	Utilize discipline-specific types of evidence.

We think that the ACT does a good job of engaging students in writing about topics that are likely to matter to them. Additionally, the topics that the ACT incorporates vary in terms of the evidence that students may include. Students might choose to use evidence learned in biology or health class about nutrition, or they might focus on the role of government in people's lives.

Stage 2 Reflection

Is this assessment approach one that you use in your classroom? How do you gauge the progress students are making in their ability to respond to audience, task, purpose, and discipline? How do you ask them to reflect upon and assess their own learning?

Stage 3: Instructional Procedures

In our experience, the key to helping students know how to respond effectively to varying demands of audience, task, purpose, and discipline is designing prompts that ask them to write for authentic audiences about varied topics. Once again, service learning provides an effective means for developing these skills.

In *The Complete Guide to Service Learning,* Kaye (2010) asserts, "When students have a sense of purpose and know someone is depending on them for the research, the incentive for grades and meeting basic expectations may be replaced with an intrinsic desire to help a person or cause" (p. 36). Students transfer the knowledge they develop through their reading to action related to a genuine need. Guilfoile and Ryan (2013) remind us that "if students do not have numerous opportunities to use content knowledge to solve interesting problems, grapple with key questions and issues of the discipline, and examine social issues, they will be unlikely to perform well on the common assessments" (p. 3).

The following lesson scenario incorporates service learning and provides a frame for talking about instructional techniques that relate to responding to varying demands of audience, task, purpose, and discipline.

SAMPLE LESSON SCENARIO
Presenting Human Rights Research

Maureen's class took part in human rights issues research with the aim of using their findings to convince others to take action. The students chose a topic with national or global significance, such as inequalities in the U.S. school system, restrictions on freedom of expression in China, and the exploitation of child soldiers in various regions around the world. Maureen asked her students to read sources with two objectives in mind: (1) to gather information and (2) to analyze how each source presented information in an effective manner.

The students conducted their research, developed outlines, and then wrote full research papers to communicate their findings. They also used their research findings to create "takeaway" items (informational brochures and flyers), applying insights they picked up from analyzing how advertisers capture the attention of audiences and use language and graphics to succinctly and effectively convey a message. The students presented their research and distributed their takeaways in several different ways. Some spoke at a local town hall meeting, others spoke with local college students or made presentations to younger students, and still others set up information booths at parents night.

The important factor was that students' work was not just written for a teacher to grade; it was written to encourage an authentic audience to take action. Once students decided to whom they would present and how, they had to consider how best to reach that audience. Based on their purpose and audience, they had to choose powerful language and incorporate specific, convincing evidence to make a strong and motivational case.

Figure 4.1 presents an overview of students' learning experience during this lesson.

FIGURE 4.1

Assignment Guide: Applying Research Findings

HUMAN RIGHTS RESEARCH

OVERVIEW

This year we have focused on the theme of power and corruption. Now it is time to investigate this theme as it connects to the current state of our world. For this project, you will research groups of people who are being treated inhumanely and the efforts of agencies that are taking action to effect change for these groups.

PRODUCTS

You will be responsible for the following: (1) Investigating valid sources on your topic for information and as models of writing style. (2) Synthesizing these sources in a coherent three- to five-page research paper. (3) Creating a brochure or flyer for distribution. (4) Presenting your findings to the community.

TIME LINE

Date	Classwork	Due at the End of the Period
Mon. 4/28	Investigate possible topics at www.amnesty.org	Three topic choices
Tues. 4/29–Thurs. 5/1	Conduct library research	Four sources identified (at least one book)
Mon. 5/5–Tues. 5/6	Note taking and outlining	Four sources, cited and annotated
Wed. 5/7–Thurs. 5/8	Outlining	Outlines
Mon. 5/12–Thurs. 5/15	Typing	Final brochure or flyer
Fri. 5/16	—	Rough draft of paper

RESEARCH OUTLINE

I. **Background/History**

　　A. Major players

　　　　Who is being treated inhumanely?

　　　　Who is mistreating this group?

　　B. Time Line

　　　　When did this begin?

　　　　Important events that led to what is happening today

FIGURE 4.1 (*continued*)
Assignment Guide: Applying Research Findings

II. Current State of Affairs

   A. Recent event that connects to this issue: _____.

      1. Who was involved?

      2. What happened?

      3. Statistics

   B. Recent event that connects to this issue: _____.

      1. Who was involved?

      2. What happened?

      3. Statistics

III. Action

   A. How are we in the United States addressing this issue?

      1. Describe a group that is addressing the issue (government, not-for-profit?).

      2. Describe its course of action.

   B. *If the violation of human rights is in another country*—Is the United Nations involved? What is the country's government doing?

      1. Describe the committee.

      2. Describe its course of action.

   C. What can we do to address this issue?

      1. What campaigns can we join or petitions can we sign?

      2. What new action can we take?

Connecting the Lesson with the CLI

Here's what this lesson looks like through the lens of Capacity 3—*respond to audience, task, purpose, and discipline:*

CLI Skill Components	Lesson Components
Recognize how tone and connotation affect meaning.	Students analyze how researchers use tone and connotation to present their findings effectively. Students analyze the ways that advertisers use tone and connotation and then develop their own social issues pamphlets and brochures based on the effective approaches they derive from the models.
Utilize discipline-specific types of evidence.	Students write a research paper and develop a presentation on a social issue of importance to them, utilizing the evidence they find in their research.

Guiding Students' Development: Skills and Strategies

Let's consider ways to guide students toward independence with each of the skills needed for this capacity.

Recognize how tone and connotation affect meaning

Connotation is a scary word. It really does connote something far more complicated than it actually means. But once students have an understanding of connotation and how it relates to tone and meaning, they quickly become experts at analyzing and employing it effectively. Here are some strategies that can call students' attention to how tone and connotation affect meaning during communication.

Playing with Voice

Every once in a while, when Maureen's students are particularly whiny, she will put on the *Oh, my God! Why is she beeeeeing like thiiiiiis?!* voice. If you need more explanation, think of a Kardashian or a Valley girl, and you'll have the sound of it in your ears. "The voice" breaks some of the tension, and it also helps Maureen's students reflect on how they sound to her. (Believe it or not, she has had classes actually ask her to do the voice because it sounds so ridiculous, and it makes them laugh.) Just as Maureen can show her students how different vocal tones and word choices affect their perception of her and what she is saying, she wants them to recognize how their tone and word choices affect their audience's perception of them.

The simplest way to do this (beyond trying "the voice," of course) is to assign students a short writing piece that they need to tailor for several different audiences. A simple written request is a great place to start: "I need permission to miss _____ because _____." The idea is to have the class consider how this request would differ depending on who is being asked: a teacher, a parent, a coach, a friend? What might change about the reasons given or the kind of words used? What difference would gender make—a boy asking a male friend versus a female friend? A girl asking a female friend versus a male friend? How might cultural background influence the way a student would ask his or her parents for permission? Would it change the reasons the students choose? Would it lead them to use a more demanding or deferential tone? Call out sets of different permission scenarios with different audiences, and give students 20 seconds or so to scribble a response. Then go back to discuss and compare what they've all written.

This activity quickly and simply addresses the concepts of recognizing how different audiences may perceive different meanings and using appropriate language and strategies for communication, and it provides students with a safe, low-pressure means of reflecting on effective communication.

Differentiation highlights/tips: Playing with Voice, when it's a spoken activity like Maureen engages in, gives students an auditory cue that helps them understand how language shifts tone. When this strategy is deployed as a writing activity, ELLs may benefit from a word bank to help them develop different kinds of writing pieces making a request to different people. For students who would benefit from additional challenge, extend the activity by asking them to create request statements that would be appropriate for additional audiences.

Advertising Analysis

Evaluating how advertisements are crafted to entice or persuade a particular audience focuses students on the ways that voice can be deployed. You may choose to concentrate solely on language, but we have found it more beneficial to have students take in the whole picture and reflect on not just the wording but also color choices, images, music, and the "star power" incorporated into various ads. This can be done fairly simply by supplying students with a selection of print ads, or you can give them the opportunity to use their cell phones or digital cameras to capture images of ads that they see in their community, their school, and their reading (in print or online). With either approach, provide students the opportunity to share an ad via a projector or the class website and lead their classmates in a discussion and analysis of their chosen ad. Figure 4.2 is an organizer that helps students analyze advertisements.

Differentiation highlights/tips: Using an Advertising Analysis organizer that includes examples provides all students with a clear model of expectations (you can provide more examples or fewer, depending on student readiness). Note that the Advertising Analysis strategy works best for ELLs when it requires analysis of visual and auditory components along with analysis of language. You can also make this a paired activity in which one student concentrates on the words and phrases and the other on image and layout choices.

FIGURE 4.2
Advertising Analysis Organizer

Advertisement name/description:

Purpose of the advertisement:

Intended audience:

Powerful words/phrases • *Example: "Just do it!"*	Effects on the audience • *Example: Makes buyers think that buying the sneakers will get them out the door and exercising*
Powerful images/layout choices	Effects on the audience

Other important notes:

Language Awareness

This activity can be both fun and extremely informative for students. At the same time that it focuses them on the power of word choice, it provides opportunities to delve into interesting topics. Begin by finding two articles that present polar sides of an issue. The "Room for Debate" section of the *New York Times*'s online Opinions page (www.nytimes.com/roomfordebate) is a particularly good resource. Ask students to analyze the language used in each article and decide how that language influences the tone of the work. For example, in a debate over using the colors pink and blue to market toys to children of different genders, Jim Silver (2014) writes, "We love to pick on Barbie for being too skinny and for having an unrealistic body type (forgetting it's a toy!), but ignore many of the 'beefed up' bodies in the action figure aisle that are equally impossible to achieve" (para. 3). Students might highlight Silver's use of the phrase "beefed up" and make a note in the margin about how its use emphasizes a body type that is equally unrealistic for males. Consider polling students for the top two most powerful words or phrases in each article and discussing their answers.

Differentiation highlights/tips: You can adapt this activity by assigning articles based on reading level difficulty or by selecting articles that address issues that are in the news or that would be particularly interesting to your students. You can also do a read-aloud of an article and model how you would critique its language.

Utilize discipline-specific types of evidence

For a long time now, many of us have been hearing that "all content-area teachers must be literacy teachers." Today's testing is finally reflecting this assertion, with many tests requiring students to use discipline-specific evidence to support claims in their writing. The following instructional strategies will help students strengthen this skill.

Liar, Liar!

A simple step toward utilizing evidence in writing is being prepared to use it in class. When a student makes a statement, Maureen will sometimes respond with a lighthearted "Liar!" Her students recognize this as a cue to present some kind of evidence for whatever statement they have just made. For instance, if a student says that George from *Of Mice and Men* is mean, she must support that statement with evidence like "George is mean because he curses at Lennie" or "because he bosses Lennie around." Then, after the first student shares evidence, Maureen invites others to counter or support it with evidence of their own. For instance: "George curses at Lennie not because he's mean but because he is frustrated after taking care of him for so long. He bosses Lenny around to keep him safe." Regularly requiring students to come up with evidence to back their claims strengthens their critical thinking about what they are reading and discussing, regardless of the subject area or whether the text is literature or an expository source.

If you use the Liar, Liar! strategy in your classroom, be sure that your students understand the rules of the game beforehand (i.e., they know you're not actually calling them a liar; you're prompting them to provide evidence).

Differentiation highlights/tips: If students struggle to provide evidence for a statement, you can give them the opportunity to ask a peer for support. Alternatively, you might offer several facts from the text as options for support.

Source Analysis

Students need to be critical consumers of information before they can decide what information is "good enough" to include in their own writing. The Source Analysis organizer in Figure 4.3 is similar to the Advertising Analysis organizer we looked at earlier. Students can easily transition to using a planner like this to guide

FIGURE 4.3
Source Analysis Organizer

Source name/description:

Author's purpose:

Intended audience:

Powerful words/phrases	Effects on the audience
• *Example: "We love to pick on Barbie for being too skinny and for having an unrealistic body type (forgetting it's a toy!), but ignore many of the "beefed up" bodies in the action figure aisle that are equally impossible to achieve" (para. 3).*	• *Example: Uses "beefed up" to create an image of the unrealistic male body type.*

Powerful statistics	Impactful anecdotes
• *Example: "LEGO introduced its LEGO Friends line to attract more girls, to resounding success" (para. 2)* NOTE: Per Bloomberg.com, sales increase that year (2013) was 25 percent.	• *Example: "Since I've been working in the toy business for more than 25 years, I am often asked, 'What should I buy my daughter or son?' My usual response is something like, "Does your daughter like Hot Wheels? Or does your son like activity or cooking toys?" The days of applying a gender to a toy are declining."*

Indications of bias:

Other notes:

their critical thinking about sources. The key understanding you want them to come to is that all information deserves scrutiny. When they find material that seems relevant, it's important for them to consider how it is presented and whether there are signs of author bias.

Differentiation highlights/tips: The Source Analysis organizer helps students think about evidence that they may want to include in their writing. As we've noted with other organizers, having examples helps to set clear expectations for all students and provides clarification for ELLs. Providing the categories (powerful words/phrases, powerful statistics, impactful anecdotes) helps to scaffold students as they engage in the close reading of their sources. You can increase the complexity of Source Analysis activities by providing different versions of the organizer with additional prompts, such as one asking students to compare the features of multiple sources.

Interdisciplinary Thinking Concept Map

When we teach teachers, we often encourage them to develop interdisciplinary plans. This is good practice for supporting transfer of ideas and skills from one subject to another. Rather than providing your students with instruction where the connections have already been overtly made for them, challenge them to make these interdisciplinary connections themselves. Ask them to create a web or mind map in which the main topic of a paper they're working on sits at the center, with various pieces of content-area evidence branching from it. Figure 4.4 shows a mind map of a response to an ACT prompt about whether schools should require all students to take a sex education course.

Differentiation highlights/tips: The Interdisciplinary Thinking Concept Map encourages all learners to think about the ways that topics and skills transfer across subject areas. You can adjust this activity to appeal to student interest by allowing students to choose which subject areas to include on the map, and you may

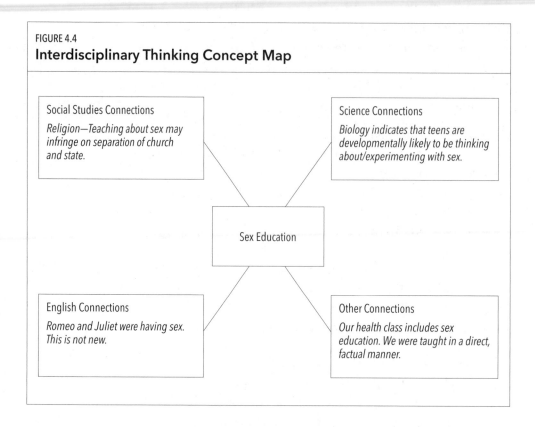

FIGURE 4.4
Interdisciplinary Thinking Concept Map

Social Studies Connections

Religion—Teaching about sex may infringe on separation of church and state.

Science Connections

Biology indicates that teens are developmentally likely to be thinking about/experimenting with sex.

Sex Education

English Connections

Romeo and Juliet were having sex. This is not new.

Other Connections

Our health class includes sex education. We were taught in a direct, factual manner.

want to provide different versions of the map to accommodate different readiness levels: partially complete maps to support ELLs or struggling learners, or maps requiring more than four connections for students who would benefit from extension.

Test Connection

Let's think back to the ACT writing prompt that we reviewed at the beginning of the chapter. Figure 4.5 outlines the CLI components that this prompt is assessing, the construct of the assessment that is measuring each component, and teaching strategies that may help prepare students for success with each component.

FIGURE 4.5

Developing Awareness of Audience, Task, Purpose, and Discipline: Skill Components, Demands of the Test, and Classroom Strategies

CLI Skill Components	Demands of the Test	Classroom Strategies
Recognize how tone and connotation affect meaning.	According to the rubric, students must show "a good command of language. Sentences are varied and word choice is varied and precise."	Playing with Voice Language Awareness Advertising Analysis
Utilize discipline-specific types of evidence.	Students will use varied evidence based on the prompt.	Liar, Liar! Source Analysis Interdisciplinary Thinking Concept Map

Stage 3 Reflection

What activities, instruction, sources, and methods would promote your students' understanding, interest, and excellence in this literacy capacity? How do the lessons you use now and the strategies you currently employ to help your students respond to audience, task, purpose, and discipline parallel the instructional procedures presented in this chapter? What changes might you make?

Many of the strategies in this chapter not only pertain to developing awareness of audience, task, purpose, and discipline but also begin to touch on the components of understanding and crafting an effective argument. Ultimately, all writing comes down to argument; it's about making claims, supporting those claims with evidence and reasoning, and doing so in a way that will connect with our readers. In the next two chapters, we examine critical thinking and valuing evidence—skills that enable students to develop effective arguments.

5

Comprehending as
well as Critiquing

*Students are engaged and open-minded—but discerning—readers and
listeners. They work diligently to understand precisely what an author
or speaker is saying, but they also question an author's or speaker's
assumptions and premises and assess the veracity of claims and the
soundness of reasoning. (CCSSI, 2015)*

In this chapter, we turn to ways to help students learn to both
read and listen closely so that they grasp the author's or speaker's message, meaning, or intent *and* apply evaluative criteria to
assess those assertions.

The ability to evaluate the ideas in a written or verbal text—
the types of critical thinking and argument skills related to this
ability—are the keys to independent thinking and decision making, and developing students' critical thinking skills is recognized
as a key goal in education (ACT, 2009; Marin & Halpern, 2011).
That so many high school seniors struggle to make informed,
thoughtful, critical judgments about written texts should give us
pause (Perie, Grigg, & Donahue, 2005). It's a common complaint
among faculty in higher education institutions that students
enter their classrooms without the necessary argument-related

skills. These students don't necessarily perform poorly in academic subjects, but their ability and inclination to engage in inferencing, in problem solving, and in forming, analyzing, and evaluating arguments is judged to be lacking. We see this among our undergraduate students, who experience a steep learning curve when it comes to engaging in critical thinking.

What can middle and high school teachers do to support the development of this capacity and ensure that our students graduate with the ability to comprehend text as well as critique it? Let's take a look.

Stage 1: Desired Results

In order for students to *comprehend as well as critique*—that is, develop textual understanding and comprehension and critical thinking skills, they must be able to

1. Question an author's assumptions and premises.
2. Assess the veracity of claims and soundness of reasoning.

Stage 1 Reflection

Are you deliberately pursuing these outcomes in your instruction now? Pick out a few lessons that have these skills among the objectives and reflect on the methods and strategies that you are using to promote students' development of these skills. Are there other skills you see as essential to comprehending as well as critiquing?

Stage 2: Evidence

Here is a sample test item from PARCC that aligns with developing students' comprehension and evaluation skills. Consider what elements of this testing you might incorporate into your classroom. How would you do so?

SAMPLE TEST ITEM
PARCC Research Simulation Task, Grade 10

In 1968 three students in Des Moines, Iowa, arrived at their separate schools wearing black armbands to protest United States involvement in the Vietnam War. The principals of the schools quickly instituted a policy banning the wearing of armbands, leading to the suspension of the students. A lawsuit filed on behalf of the students was eventually argued in the Supreme Court on November 12, 1968. Today you will read two passages and listen to a short audio clip discussing the context and impact of the case. At the end of the task, you will be asked to write an analytical essay.

Source: PARCC, 2015b, p. 16.

Let's look at how this task relates to the CLI's description of what it means to develop comprehension and evaluation skills:

Demands of the Text	CLI Skill Components
Students analyze the information presented in articles and an audio clip.	Question an author's assumptions and premises.
Students write an essay analyzing the information in the sources.	Assess the veracity of claims and soundness of reasoning.

This research simulation task from PARCC clearly requires students to go beyond understanding what they're reading; they also have to engage in higher-order thinking in order to analyze and evaluate their sources.

Stage 2 Reflection

Is this assessment approach one that you use in your classroom? How do you gauge the progress students are making in their ability to comprehend as well as critique? How do you ask them to reflect upon and assess their own learning?

Stage 3: Instructional Procedures

In our experience, students can engage in meaningful conversations and writing about texts they are reading but still have difficulty analyzing and evaluating such texts and developing reflective and thoughtful, evidence-based ideas and opinions. The thinking required here goes beyond recalling; it involves a consideration of multiple perspectives to form sound judgments supported by logical arguments.

According to the research, explicit instruction is an effective method of developing students' critical thinking skills (Halpern, 2001; Lai, 2011; Marin & Halpern, 2011). In addition, studies have found that collaborative learning opportunities improve students' critical thinking dispositions and motivate them to increase their intellectual skills (Karami, Pekmehr, & Aghili, 2012; Lai, 2011). Therefore, we recommend combining explicit instruction on how to comprehend and critique texts effectively with opportunities for students to engage in such deep analysis and evaluation in collaborative situations.

The following sample lesson scenario illustrates this approach and provides a frame for talking about instructional techniques that foster the ability to comprehend as well as critique.

SAMPLE LESSON SCENARIO
Analyzing Sources

Vicky's class had just finished reading and discussing the novel *Of Mice and Men* by John Steinbeck. Students were interested in the ending and wanted to explore further the moral question it raises: "Is it ever justifiable for someone to take a person's life in order to prevent suffering, whether with or without that person's voluntary consent?" To do so, they engaged in an in-depth study of euthanasia.

It began with students participating in an Improvised Debate (see p. 79) and arguing both sides of the issue. Two volunteers presented arguments based on their current knowledge and assumptions, without having read any additional information on the topic. The class

SAMPLE LESSON SCENARIO (*continued*)
Analyzing Sources

discussed the veracity of these assumptions. At this point, it was time for students to become more informed about different perspectives on euthanasia by reading, viewing, analyzing, and evaluating print and multimedia sources.* They watched a "Right to Die" video, explored a website that advocates for hope and life, read blog posts presenting both sides of the issue, and read an opinion article supporting assisted suicide.

Vicky guided her students to think critically about the information they were taking in, analyze what the sources revealed about the authors' assumptions, and evaluate the authors' reasoning. To wrap up this study, students created and shared digital presentations synthesizing the information in the four types of sources.

*The sources students read in this lesson scenario are expository texts, but the lesson design and strategies here can be easily adapted to examine literature.

Connecting the Lesson with the CLI

Let's look at this lesson through the lens of the target CLI—*comprehend as well as critique:*

CLI Skill Components	Lesson Components
Question an author's assumptions and premises.	Students improvise a debate where they question the speakers' assumptions and premises.
	Students view a video and read a website, blog posts, and an opinion article related to a common issue.
Assess the veracity of claims and soundness of reasoning.	Students critique the sources provided.

Guiding Students' Development: Skills and Strategies

Now we'll consider how to guide students as they work toward developing each skill within this literacy capacity.

Question an author's assumptions and premises

In order to question an author's assumptions and premises in a written or verbal text, students must first understand the information the text is communicating and analyze its presentation. The following instructional strategies can help students develop skills with textual comprehension and analysis of arguments.

Improvised Debate

Improvised Debate helps students recognize the importance of strong evidence and of counterargument, and provides valuable formative information for the teacher in the process. As the name implies, this activity presents a contrast to the carefully planned Debate strategy (see p. 53) in that students work out their arguments on the fly. Two students or two pairs of students stand in front of the room and improvise an argument over a controversial topic (e.g., euthanasia). They may or may not have prior knowledge about the topic, but what they say can provide excellent insight into what they know about successful argumentation.

This activity also offers an opportunity for the rest of the class to evaluate the claims and reasoning on display. While the volunteers are debating, the seated students take notes on strong arguments, evidence, and counterarguments. Each argument should take only three to five minutes. Afterward, the teacher leads students in a longer reflective activity in which they use their notes to discuss the strengths of each argument.

Differentiation highlights/tips: Improvised Debate can be a way to get even the most reluctant students to try their hand at acting without the pressure of having to memorize and perform a script. They pretend to be a true believer in their assigned stance and give it all they've got. Even though improvisation is a feature of this strategy, students who cannot easily think on the spot can benefit from some prep time. In addition, consider providing partial scripts with key points or language choices to students needing that support, including ELLs.

MAAPP CEnteR

The inelegantly written but very helpful MAAPP CEnteR strategy (see Figure 5.1) is a scaffolding process that guides students' critical evaluation of a text. With a prepared "map" of analysis prompts in hand, students navigate an article, video, website, blog post, and so on by considering the author's *m*ain points, *a*udience, *a*ssumptions, *p*erspective, *p*urpose, *c*laims, *e*vidence, and *r*esults. It's a dissection involving both interpretation and inference, and it elevates students' thinking about the author's work to a higher cognitive level.

Differentiation highlights/tips: MAAPP CEnteR's guiding questions and sentence starters provide built-in support, but you might have students work through the activity in pairs or small groups. You can also divide the class into eight groups, assign one question to each group, and then have all the groups share their responses.

Point of View Writing

What assumptions and premises are driving the author of a text? Point of View Writing prompts students to explore this question by—you guessed it—writing from different points of view. For example, if the topic is euthanasia, how might the thoughts of a doctor or social worker compare to the thoughts of someone who is witnessing a friend suffer from a terminal illness? When students deliberately write from different perspectives, they become more aware of the biases that different authors may have.

Differentiation highlights/tips: Point of View Writing raises students' awareness and sensitivity about different points of view, some of which may be rooted in culture. You might extend this strategy by having students work in pairs to share their *own* points of view on a topic and articulate how their culture (and by culture, we mean everything about them) informs their

FIGURE 5.1
MAAPP CEnteR Analysis

Questioning an Author's Assumptions and Premises

Directions: Respond to the following questions based on the text you are listening to, viewing, or reading.

Title of Text:

Main Ideas
1. What are the main ideas of the text?
The three main ideas of the text are . . .
    1.
    2.
    3.

Audience
2. Who is the intended audience?
The author has written this text for . . .

Assumptions
3. What are the author's assumptions—i.e., what facts are taken for granted?
The author generalizes and does not seem to believe it's necessary to address . . .

Purpose
4. What is the author's purpose in creating this content?
The author's intent is to . . .

Perspective
5. What is the author's perspective on this topic?
The author believes that . . .

Claims
6. What claims does the author make?
The author asserts that . . .

Evidence
7. What evidence does the author provide (facts and experiences)?
Two facts and experiences that the author presents are . . .
    1.
    2.

Results
8. What are the results (implications or effects of the author's thinking)?
Two consequences of the author's thinking are . . .
    1.
    2.

perspective. By encouraging students to better understand who they are, we support their ability to understand who others are. This is especially important in culturally diverse classrooms. Personalization also increases student motivation to write. Allowing students to choose the point of view they'll use in their writing is another way to differentiate.

Assess the veracity of claims and soundness of reasoning

If you just ask students to evaluate a piece of writing, many will not know where to begin. Some might produce a superficial summary or just present an analysis of the main ideas and details without bringing evaluative criteria into the equation. According to Bloom, evaluation is the highest form of cognitive activity, so it is no surprise that some students may struggle with it. Here are some strategies to advance students' powers of evaluation.

Think Aloud

Because the evaluation of writing is so difficult, it may help students to see you struggle through this process. Read an article aloud to students and ask questions of the author as you go. What information needs more support? What logical fallacies can you query? If possible, project the text on the board so you can model the criteria you apply and how you annotate the text as you interact with it.

Differentiation highlights/tips: Think Aloud is a way to have students observe other ways of approaching and evaluating a text. While you are thinking aloud, you can have students take notes on what you are saying and the questions you are asking. Have them identify patterns in your approach. Call on students to model their own thinking, an activity that promotes their metacognition. When planning to use this strategy, you might also do a dry run ahead of time and prepare a handout for your struggling learners that captures your key points and highlights your approach. You can even color-code it to call attention to your patterns of thought. Also consider recording Think Alouds (audio or video) and making them available for students to replay with a copy of the text in front of them.

Scaffolded Critique

The Scaffolded Critique strategy (see Figure 5.2) supports students as they go through the evaluation process. With a prepared form in front of them, they read a short text and engage in summary, analysis, and evaluation. Specific questions prompt them to consider the text's main ideas and its strengths and weaknesses and also provide them with guidelines for (or reminders of) how to present their own evidence-supported opinions of the text's content and style.

FIGURE 5.2
Scaffolded Critique

Content Summary and Analysis

Directions: Summarize and analyze the author's ideas in the article.

1. What are the author's main ideas (assumptions, claims, reasoning)? Discuss one or two main ideas.
2. What is the supporting evidence?

TIP: Think about the length of your paper—two pages. Be concise! Only include relevant main ideas and details.

Content Evaluation

Directions: Evaluate the author's ideas in the article. Consider the following factors (adapted from Rosen & Behrens, 2014), then respond to questions 1 and 2.

- Is the author a respected authority? How do you know?
- Is the source current? What is the copyright/publication date?
- What is the author claiming?
- Are the author's claims logical?
- Are the author's claims accurate?
- What is the evidence? How does the evidence support the author's claims?

(continued)

FIGURE 5.2 (*continued*)
Scaffolded Critique

- Is the article well organized, clear, and easy to understand?
- Is the article appropriate for the intended audience?
- Have important words been defined and explained?
- Does the author leave any questions unanswered? What questions?
- Is the author fair to all points of view?

1. What are the strengths of the article in terms of the author's ideas (assumptions, assertions, claims, reasoning, or evidence)? Discuss one or two strengths.

2. What are the weaknesses of the article in terms of the author's ideas (assumptions, assertions, claims, reasoning, or evidence)? Discuss one or two weaknesses.

TIP: If, in your opinion, the article has no weaknesses, think about and write more questions that this author or other authors writing about the topic could address.

Reaction
Directions: Discuss your reactions to the author's ideas:

1. What is your overall opinion of the author's ideas?
2. What does the article make you think about?
3. Are there any ideas that evoke a strong response from you? Elaborate.
4. What connections can you make to yourself or to other texts or to life?
5. What are the implications of the author's ideas?
6. What questions does the article raise that could be answered in future research?

TIP: Be thoughtful. Consider carefully what you want to convey. Don't just write about your personal experiences and stop there; write about how your experiences apply to the larger picture.

Writing Style Checks:
1. Is your summary concise?
2. Is your writing clear?
3. Does your critique include headings?
4. Are your paragraphs well developed?
5. Do you use appropriate transitions?
6. Is your writing style formal?
7. Have you followed the ELA conventions (punctuation, capitalization, subject-verb agreement, verb tense, etc.) and double-checked to correct any errors?
8. Do you use past tense to refer to the ideas in the article and keep the verb tense consistent throughout?
9. Are your citations correct?
10. Does your critique consist of the required number of paragraphs or pages?

FIGURE 5.2 (*continued*)

Scaffolded Critique

More Tips for Writing a Critique

✓ Write your critique in essay form. Avoid using the organizational structure of the author's article, because following the same structure makes you more likely to produce a summary than an analysis.

✓ Begin with an introduction that defines the subject of your critique and your point of view.

✓ Defend your point of view by raising specific issues or analyses of the argument(s).

✓ Conclude your critique by summarizing your argument and reemphasizing your opinion.

✓ Identify and explain the author's ideas. Include specific passages that support your description of the author's point of view.

✓ Offer your evaluation: (1) Explain what you think about the author's argument; (2) describe several points with which you agree or disagree.

✓ Provide evidence: For each of the points you mention, include specific passages from the text (summarized, quoted, or paraphrased) that provide evidence for your point of view. Be sure to explain how the passages support your point of view.

✓ Draw your conclusion(s): What are the implications? What research remains to be done?

Thank you to Dr. Audrey Cohan for providing information that influenced the development of this handout.

Differentiation highlights/tips: Scaffolded Critique gives students prompts and elements to think about to help them write a critique. Because you design the scaffold, you can tailor it to the needs of your students and the objectives of your assignment. This might mean providing more or fewer questions that are more or less detailed. You can also incorporate some of the questions in an essay frame to help students organize their writing. You might want to show model essays to provide an idea of what a good critique looks like, but be careful not to provide exemplars that are far beyond students' present reach; know their current abilities and offer model essays that they could actually write themselves.

Guided Peer Response

Peer response is a familiar strategy that involves students evaluating one another's work and giving and receiving direct, constructive feedback. However, every teacher has had the experience of students giving peer feedback that consists of one-word responses (e.g., "Good"). The Guided Peer Response strategy involves distributing a list of specific questions that ask for explanations. With this additional direction, students are more likely to produce responses that are on target and helpful, and they get practice applying evaluative criteria. The question set in Figure 5.3 provides a model.

FIGURE 5.3
Guided Peer Response Question Set

Directions: Use these questions to guide your evaluation of your partner's critique of the article we read.

1. Is the critique written in essay form?
2. Does the critique begin with an introduction that defines the subject of the critique?
3. Does the critique include the major arguments presented in the article?
4. Does the critique include the supporting evidence for the arguments presented in the article?
5. Does the critique note one or two strengths in the article?
6. Does the critique include one or two weaknesses in the article?
7. Does the critic explain what he or she thinks about the arguments in the article?
8. Does the critic provide evidence for his or her opinion by citing specific passages from the text?
9. Does the critique include a conclusion?
10. Is the critique well written? If yes, give two or three examples to support this conclusion. If no, give two or three suggestions of how the critique could be improved.

Differentiation highlights/tips: When setting up Guided Peer Response pairs, you can group students homogenously or heterogeneously, according to their abilities, strengths, interests, learning styles, and so on. You can also limit the number of questions or evidence for students who are struggling with the content or work more slowly, or include illustrative examples of good feedback (e.g., "List one suggestion for improvement [for example: 'The author needs to give one or two more examples that support the stated claim that euthanasia devalues human life.']").

Test Connection

Figure 5.4 provides an overview of the CLI skill components featured in this chapter's excerpt from a PARCC exam, how the task is measuring each component, and the teaching strategies we recommend to help students build those skills.

FIGURE 5.4

Comprehending as well as Critiquing:
Skill Components, Demands of the Test, and Strategies

CLI Skill Components	Demands of the Test	Teaching Strategies
Question an author's assumptions and premises.	Students analyze the information presented in articles and an audio clip.	Improvised Debate MAAPP CEnteR Point of View Writing
Assess the veracity of claims and soundness of reasoning.	Students write an essay analyzing the information in the sources.	Think Aloud Scaffolded Critique Guided Peer Response

Stage 3 Reflection

What activities, instruction, sources, and methods would promote your students' understanding, interest, and excellence in this literacy capacity? How do the lessons you use now and the strategies you currently employ to help your students comprehend as well as critique parallel the instructional procedures presented in this chapter? What changes might you make?

Throughout this chapter, we have focused on means for supporting students in questioning authors' assumptions and questioning the evidence authors provide. For some students, this does not come easily; they are used to trusting that what they are told and believing that what they hear or read is "the truth." This is a problem not only because colleges and careers will expect them to be critical thinkers but also because they live in an age where technology has opened the door to multiple diverse perspectives that require careful consideration. In today's world, authorship and authority have been radically democratized via social media, comments sections, and blogs, and students need to be able to evaluate the voices they will encounter in text, online, and in the media (mainstream, social, and fringe). They need to know how to sift through various voices and discern the truth so that they can develop their *own* voice.

The sources students read in this chapter's lesson scenario are expository texts, but the lesson design and strategies used can be easily adapted to examine literature. The next capacity we explore—valuing evidence—focuses more specifically on fostering students' critical thinking for literary analysis.

6

Valuing Evidence

Students cite specific evidence when offering an oral or written inter-pretation of a text. They use relevant evidence when supporting their own points in writing and speaking, making their reasoning clear to the reader or listener, and they constructively evaluate others' use of evidence. (CCSSI, 2015)

In this chapter, we explore methods and strategies that help students value and use evidence in their written and spoken communication.

The College Board makes a strong case for the importance of this CLI:

> Students' abilities to analyze source texts and, more broadly, to under-stand and make effective use of evidence in reading and writing are widely recognized as central to college and career readiness. National curriculum surveys conducted by the College Board and others dem-onstrate that postsecondary instructors rate high in importance such capacities as . . . recognizing logical flaws in an author's argument, as well as writing analyses and evaluations of texts, using supporting details and examples, and developing a logical argument . . . [Universities] have devoted considerable resources to developing the skills of source analy-sis and evidence use in their students. (College Board, 2014b, p. 2)

We agree that these skills are important. Of course, the trend in ELA classrooms when we began teaching 20 years ago was to teach literature rather than to teach reading—meaning that we would set a schedule to teach a certain number of works of literature each year. We would help students deconstruct the meaning of the chosen works, and apart from making thematic links or the occasional connections regarding writing style, it was clearly the *works* that were the main focus. If you asked students what they were learning in English class, they would answer with the title of the book that they were reading rather than with a set of skills or a thematic focus.

According to Hill (2011), the literature approach to ELA is based on an assumption that "once a student can comprehend one text, he or she can comprehend anything. But in reality, this is not the case. Each time a student tackles a text that increases in complexity, the need for instruction escalates" (para. 12). As lovers of many great books, we do not want to turn away from guiding our students through challenging literature. But we *do* want to ensure students see how they are developing and transferring critical skills as they move through those texts with us.

In general, then, what can middle and high school teachers do to ensure our students graduate with the skills they need to identify, use, and value evidence in their communication? Once again, we will use the backward design model to focus our planning.

Stage 1: Desired Results

We looked over the description of this CLI and found two key descriptors. In order to *value evidence,* students must be able to

1. Constructively evaluate others' use of evidence.
2. Use relevant evidence.

Stage 1 Reflection

Are you deliberately pursuing these outcomes in your instruction now? Pick out a few lessons that have these skills among the objectives and reflect on the methods and strategies that you are using to promote students' development of these skills. Are there other skills you see as essential to valuing evidence?

Stage 2: Evidence

To get a sense of how test makers are assessing students' ability to understand how evidence is and can be used in written and spoken arguments, let's look at an analytical task from the SAT.

SAMPLE TEST ITEM

SAT Analytical Task

As you read the passage below, consider how Dana Gioia [the author] uses

- Evidence, such as facts or examples to support claims.
- Reasoning to develop ideas and to connect claims and evidence.
- Stylistic or persuasive elements, such as word choice or appeals to emotion, to add power to the ideas expressed.

Source: College Board, 2015c, p. 77.

Here is a closer look at how the demands of the test relate to valuing evidence as described in this CLI:

Demands of the Test	CLI Skill Components
Students analyze how the author uses evidence to support claims, reasoning to develop ideas, and stylistic or persuasive elements.	Constructively evaluate others' use of evidence.
In communicating their analysis of the text, students utilize relevant evidence that they clearly relate to their claims about the writing.	Use relevant evidence.

Stage 2 Reflection

Is this assessment approach one that you use in your classroom? How do you gauge the progress students are making in their ability to value evidence? How do you ask them to reflect upon and assess their own learning?

Stage 3: Instructional Procedures

The following lesson scenario provides a frame for further discussion of instructional techniques that promote the skills associated with valuing evidence.

SAMPLE LESSON SCENARIO
Deconstructing Model Texts

After reading *Hamlet*, Maureen's students took part in a Carousel Analysis activity (see p. 93) during which they examined brief excerpts (two to three sentences) from critics' responses to the play. During the Carousel Analysis, students wrote about how the play supported the commentary by underlining a component of the critic's claim and writing a margin note that related to a plot point or quote from the play. Based on this activity and their interest in or appraisal of the critic's case, students chose a particular piece of criticism to read in full. Then they developed essays in which they analyzed their chosen critic's take on *Hamlet* in terms of claim, use of evidence, reasoning, and style.

Connecting the Lesson with the CLI

Let's look at this lesson through the lens of the CLI—*value evidence*:

CLI Skill Components	Lesson Components
Constructively evaluate others' use of evidence.	Students analyze the critic's writing.
Use relevant evidence.	Students draw on specific evidence from the critic's work and use it in their analytical essay.

Guiding Students' Development: Skills and Strategies

Now let's consider ways to guide students as they work toward independence with each of the skills needed for this capacity.

Constructively evaluate others' use of evidence

Evaluating strong models of evidence use supports students' development as critical readers and stronger writers. The following strategies help students progress toward independence in evaluating others' use of evidence.

Carousel Analysis

Create posters with excerpts of varied critics' writing at the center. The excerpts should be brief but powerful; we recommend two or three sentences. Working in small groups, students rotate among the posters, noting how these comments relate to the source text. One way to do this is to ask students to color-code their responses: use a red marker to underline powerful use of evidence, a green marker to underline strong reasoning or connection to a claim, a blue marker to underline elements of style or rhetorical appeals that are effective. We recommend requiring students to write margin notes explaining why they categorized the underlined text in such a manner—and to put their initials next to their annotations so that you can call on them for further elaboration.

Differentiation highlights/tips: The Carousel Analysis activity is especially engaging for visual and kinesthetic learners. You can support ELLs by providing prompts or sentence starters for margin notes. You can also provide a list of rhetorical devices or words/phrases associated with style in order to help ELLs or struggling learners label elements of style. Since this is a group activity, you may opt to pair nonnative speakers with native speakers.

Literature Circles

Literature Circles are an excellent way to encourage students to critically discuss a text. To connect with the elements of this particular CLI, we modified the roles that students might assume.

Figure 6.1 presents Literature Circle roles that focus specifically on valuing evidence.

FIGURE 6.1
Literature Circle Roles for Valuing Evidence

Evidence Evaluator	Reasoning Reactor
YOUR TASK: 1. Read through the text and write down what you consider to be the three to five most effective pieces of evidence that author has used. 2. Develop a question to guide your group discussion of the examples you selected.	YOUR TASK: 1. Read through the text and write down what you consider to be the three to five most effective examples of reasoning (connection of the evidence to the author's claim) utilized by the author. 2. Develop a question to guide your group discussion of the examples you selected.
Style Surveyor	**Pathos Purveyor**
YOUR TASK: 1. Read through the text and write down what you consider to be the three to five most effective examples of the author's writing style. This may include vocabulary, sentence structure, use of rhetorical questions, and so on. 2. Develop a question to guide your group discussion of the examples you selected.	YOUR TASK: 1. Read through the text and write down what you consider to be the three to five most effective examples of pathos (appeal to emotion) utilized by the author. 2. Develop a question to guide your group discussion of the examples you selected.

Differentiation highlights/tips: The Literature Circles strategy is ideal for a heterogeneous classroom because it allows you to assign roles to capitalize on students' varied natural skills or to challenge them to develop skills that need strengthening. You can also adapt the number of examples or questions that you require students to identify or provide sentence starters to help students develop questions for their group.

Source Analysis Graphic Organizer

Although this strategy has students working independently to analyze a source, it is built on a graphic organizer that provides structure and guidance (see Figure 6.2).

FIGURE 6.2

Source Analysis Graphic Organizer

Title of the source: _____

Author(s): _____

Date of publication: _____

Author's claim: _____

Evidence	Warrant
What facts, statistics, anecdotes, or other information does the author include to support the claim?	How does the author connect the evidence to the claim?
Example: Bloom highlights the speedy time line of Romeo and Juliet's relationship.	*Example: This exemplifies the idea that the intensity of their love could not have endured over a long period of time.*

Differentiation highlights/tips: A Source Analysis Graphic Organizer calls attention to the connection between evidence and an author's claims. Incorporating example responses, as Figure 6.2 does, is beneficial for students who are developing their analytical skills and for ELLs. You can include further scaffolding by providing sentence starters within the organizer. For example, you might alter the "Evidence" side to read "The critic says . . ." and the "Warrant" side to read "This connects to my claim that _____ because _____."

Use relevant evidence

Not only do students need to identify strong evidence as used by other writers, but they also need to be able to use evidence effectively in their own writing. We have found that many students struggle to articulate how the evidence that they choose relates to their claim. They can *recognize* a connection but just don't know how to *explain* that connection or incorporate the evidence into an original argument. The following strategies are good ways to support students' ability to use relevant evidence effectively.

Literary Analysis Essay Planner

The Literary Analysis Essay Planner (see Figure 6.3) is a versatile strategy that can be easily adapted for all kinds of analytical essays.

FIGURE 6.3

Literary Analysis Essay Planner

Thesis:

In _____
(title)

the author _____
(author's name)   (what does the author do?)

through _____
(list rhetorical strategies that the author employs)

in order to _____ .
(author's purpose)

Example:

In Romeo and Juliet, *William Shakespeare focuses on motifs of love and violence through plot development, characterization,*
‾‾‾
   (title)   (author's name)   (what does the author do?)   (list rhetorical strategies that the author employs)

oxymoron, and irony in order to show the ways in which these seemingly estranged concepts are often intertwined.

Evidence Cite the textual evidence that supports your thesis.	Literary/ Rhetorical Device	Warrant Tell how the evidence connects with your thesis.
Example: Romeo says after the fight in Act I, "O Brawling love, O loving hate" (1.1.166).	*Oxymoron*	*Shakespeare's use of oxymoron highlights how the concepts of violence and love are deeply intertwined. The brawl and hatred result from the love that the fighters have for their families.*

Differentiation highlights/tips: The Literary Analysis Essay Planner makes us think of the Mad Libs that we completed when we were kids. The labels beneath each line clearly state what needs to be included. You can take this scaffolding even further by reminding students to underline titles or capitalize initial letters of an author's name or the major words within titles. Like the Source Analysis Graphic Organizer, the Literary Analysis Essay Planner helps students focus on how the evidence the author presents relates to the text's claim or thesis. You can use sentence starters similar to those of the column headings of Figure 6.2 to help ELLs zero in on the evidence and warrant.

Blackout Poetry

Often students are able to identify literary devices or significant quotes from a work but struggle to determine which devices or quotes are actually relevant to a claim they want to make. Blackout Poetry is a creative way to get students to represent their thinking about a particular theme or motif in a work of literature. Once their thoughts are on the page, you could provide specific guidance or lead reflective activities that help them make connections they might otherwise have missed. There are three simple steps for students to follow: (1) select a passage that represents a theme or motif in the text; (2) highlight phrases or words from the passage that are significant to that theme or motif; and (3) create a piece of artwork that "blacks out" the rest of the passage, leaving only the highlighted words prominent for the viewer.

These instructions makes more sense when you see their outcome. Figure 6.4 shows a Blackout Poem created to highlight the theme of "brawling love" in *Romeo and Juliet*. Notice how the words that remain visible do form a sort of poem—and how the student has created artwork that conveys the chosen theme.

You might opt to require students to submit a brief explanation of the theme or motif of focus, the passages they selected, and their artistic choices for the "blackout." Just as we sometimes struggle to understand what our nine-year-olds draw for

FIGURE 6.4
A Blackout Poem: "Brawling Love" in *Romeo and Juliet*

Alas, that love, whose view is muffled still,

Should, without eyes, see pathways to his will!

Where shall we dine?—O me! What fray was here?

Yet tell me not, for I have heard it all.

Here's much to do with hate but more with love.

Why then, O brawling love, O loving hate,

O anything of nothing first created!

O heavy lightness, serious vanity,

Misshapen chaos of well-seeming forms!

Feather of lead, bright smoke, cold fire, sick health,

Still-waking sleep, that is not what it is!

This love feel I, that feel no love in this.

Dost thou not laugh?

Romeo and Juliet

(Act I, scene 1, lines 161-173)

us, you may find that you need a bit of explanation around your students' choices. This additional step is the equivalent to saying to a child, "Tell me about your picture."

Do remain open-minded as you review students' work. They may have interesting rationales for their choices. Also, remember that not all students are artists; the images they create may be more symbolic than representative.

Differentiation highlights/tips: Blackout Poetry provides an unconventional way for students to think about evidence. It is especially appealing for creative and artistic students and those with well-developed verbal-linguistic intelligence. ELLs benefit from having the freedom to choose a work that speaks most directly to them in relation to a theme.

ICE Your Quotes

Once students choose the evidence that they want to include in their writing, it's necessary that they be able to cite that evidence accurately. Many students benefit from using a mnemonic device. Whenever the assignment requires them to incorporate evidence into their writing, try reminding them to ICE (Introduce, Cite, Explain) their quotes. Though they may not always have the source information to cite properly, if they keep this mnemonic in their minds, they are more likely to remember to introduce and explain the material they want to quote.

Differentiation highlights/tips: The mnemonic ICE is a helpful reminder to ELLs and to struggling writers. Most students enjoy eating cake, and most would agree that cake tastes better with icing. Just as they would request that someone put the finishing touch on a cake by icing it, you are requesting that they put the finishing touch on their quotes by ICE-ing them. Again, a frame may help ELLs to make sure that they include all the ICE components.

Test Connection

Figure 6.5 outlines the CLI components that are being assessed in this chapter's sample SAT analytical essay prompt, the construct that is measuring each component, and teaching strategies that may help prepare students for success with each component.

FIGURE 6.5

Valuing Evidence: Skill Components, Demands of the Test, and Strategies

CLI Skill Components	Demands of the Test	Teaching Strategies
Constructively evaluate others' use of evidence.	Students analyze how the author uses evidence to support claims, reasoning to develop ideas, and stylistic or persuasive elements.	Carousel Analysis Literature Circles Source Analysis Graphic Organizer
Use relevant evidence.	In communicating their analysis of the text, students utilize relevant evidence that they clearly relate to their claims about the writing.	Literary Analysis Essay Planner Blackout Poetry ICE Your Quotes

Stage 3 Reflection

What activities, instruction, sources, and methods would promote your students' understanding, interest, and excellence in this literacy capacity? How do the lessons you use now and the strategies you currently employ to help your students value evidence parallel the instructional procedures presented in this chapter? What changes might you make?

Back in Chapter 2, we noted that reading critically and utilizing evidence effectively are the skills upon which other literacy capacities hinge. Students must be able to recognize a writer's meaning and analyze how the writer uses evidence that connects with and supports a claim to develop a strong argument. Once students become cognizant of the choices that skilled writers make, they can incorporate similar choices when they're challenged to construct arguments.

In the next chapter, we discuss how students can apply their analytical and evaluative skills surrounding evidence when they use technology and digital media.

7

Using Technology and Digital Media

Students employ technology thoughtfully to enhance their reading, writing, speaking, listening, and language use. They tailor their searches online to acquire useful information efficiently, and they integrate what they learn using technology with what they learn offline. They are familiar with the strengths and limitations of various technological tools and mediums and can select and use those best suited to their communication goals. (CCSSI, 2015)

In this chapter, we explore methods and strategies to help students develop the capacity to *use technology and digital media strategically and capably* by the time they graduate high school.

The importance of this CLI is underscored by a Pew Research study that surveyed more than 2,000 teachers about how their students use technology for research. Overall, respondents indicated that technology has a mostly positive effect on students' research abilities. However, some concerns emerged:

> [Seventy-six percent] of teachers surveyed "strongly agree" with the assertion that Internet search engines have conditioned students to expect to be able to find information quickly and easily. Large majorities also agree with the assertion that the amount of information available online today is overwhelming to most students (83%) and that today's digital technologies discourage students from using a wide range of sources when conducting research (71%). Fewer teachers,

but still a majority of this sample (60%), agree with the assertion that today's technologies make it harder for students to find credible sources of information. (Purcell et al., 2012, para. 12)

We believe that "in order to participate fully in contemporary society, our students must be able to think, create, critique, question and communicate effectively using the semiotic forms they encounter daily" (Connolly & Giouroukakis, 2011, p. 2). In our experience, although students nowadays are capable of using technology quite adeptly (iPads, social media, electronics, etc.), they still have trouble conducting research online—searching for data, determining credible sources, and synthesizing and evaluating information. They are also impatient in the research process and expect results almost instantly. That is why, when assigned an academic research paper, many typically rely on Google and other search engines to lead them to information, without taking the time to consider the trustworthiness of the sources and evidence. Or they may avoid going through the painstaking process of searching for reliable sources in the library databases. Providing opportunities for students to learn how to use technology and digital media will help them develop invaluable cognitive and problem-solving skills and prepare them to be deliberate and thoughtful consumers and users of information.

What can we do to help students develop this essential capacity of next generation literacy? Once again, the three stages of the backward design model focus us on the desired results, the evidence of mastery we're looking for, and instructional procedures to employ.

Stage 1: Desired Results

We looked over the description of this CLI and found three key descriptors. *To use technology and digital media strategically and capably*, students must be able to

1. Tailor searches online to acquire useful information efficiently.

2. Integrate technology-based learning with what is learned offline.

3. Select and use those tools best suited for communication.

Stage 1 Reflection

Are you deliberately pursuing these outcomes in your instruction now? Pick out a few lessons that have these skills among the objectives and reflect on the methods and strategies that you are using to promote students' development of these skills. Are there other skills you see as essential to using technology and visual media?

Stage 2: Evidence

To get a sense of how test makers are opting to assess students' use of technology and media, let's take a look at a sample performance task from Smarter Balanced.

SAMPLE TEST ITEM
Smarter Balanced Performance Task, Grade 11

Your task

In your economics class, you are discussing the importance of making smart financial decisions. Your teacher tells you that, in some school districts, students are required to take a financial literacy class before graduating. Your school board is hosting a meeting to decide whether to offer such a course for graduation and wants students to contribute their perspectives. As part of your initial research, you have found four sources about financial literacy classes.

After you have reviewed these sources, you will answer some questions about them. Briefly scan the sources and the three questions that follow. Then, go back and read the sources carefully so you will have the information you will need to answer the questions and finalize your research. You may click on the Global Notes button to take notes on the information you find in the sources as you read. You may also use scratch paper to take notes.

In Part 2, you will write an argumentative essay on a topic related to the sources.

Source: Smarter Balanced, 2014b, Performance Task 1.

Here is a specific look at how the demands of this test relate to the CLI's description of using technology and media strategically and capably:

Demands of the Test	CLI Skill Components
This task simulates Internet research. Students must read, evaluate, and cite as appropriate to the task.	Tailor searches online to acquire useful information efficiently.
Students may integrate what they know about the topic along with the information presented in the sources.	Integrate what is learned by using technology with what is learned offline.
Students are required to use a word processing program.	Select and use those [tools] best suited for communication.

This Smarter Balanced task parallels what would happen if students conducted an online search for information related to their topic. The prompt encourages them to consider their sources critically and to combine information from the sources and their own knowledge in order to develop an argumentative essay.

Stage 2 Reflection

Is this assessment approach one that you use in your classroom? How do you gauge the progress students are making in their ability to use technology and visual media? How do you ask them to reflect upon and assess their own learning?

Stage 3: Instructional Procedures

In our experience, students must be taught and shown that technology can be a tool for effective and efficient research and communication. At the same time, teachers need to reinforce the role that offline research, class discussions, and assignments have in supporting deeper content learning. Discerning how and when technology is most useful is the strategic component of this CLI.

The following sample lesson scenario provides a frame for talking about instructional techniques that relate to using technology and digital media strategically and capably. It offers students the opportunity to integrate information they find online with what they find in print texts and lets them decide which tools are best to communicate their learning, digital or print.

Students use their higher-order thinking skills—comprehension, analysis, synthesis, and evaluation—as they identify credible sources, comprehend what they read, put together and evaluate the information, and represent it both visually and in writing. In fact, students using well-designed combinations of visuals and text learn more than students who use only text (Fadel, 2008). The visual and the written representation part of the lesson allow students multiple ways to express their thoughts and ideas as well as to appeal to their peers' diverse ways of learning.

SAMPLE LESSON SCENARIO
Synthesizing Digital and Print Texts

Vicky's class participated in a multimodal project in which students studied the topic of global warming. She began with an activity that asked students to go through the alphabet and, for each letter, come up with a word or a phrase associated with the term *global warming*. This informal assessment helped Vicky gauge what knowledge her students already had about the topic. She then assigned them to respond to analysis questions about (1) a clip from the documentary film *An Inconvenient Truth*, (2) a political cartoon, and (3) an article about global warming. Students had to conduct online research in groups, find three credible websites that had more information about the topic, and take notes on a concept map. After mapping the print sources and the online sources (six sources in total), the students synthesized the information and represented it in one of two formats: a print Bulletin Board Display (see p. 112) or Digital Storytelling (e.g., a Photo Story; see p. 113). They also wrote an informative essay to accompany their visual presentation.

Connecting the Lesson with the CLI

Here's what this lesson looks like through the lens of the CLI—*use technology and media strategically and capably*:

CLI Skill Components	Lesson Components
Tailor searches online to acquire useful information efficiently.	Students research credible sources that contain information about global warming.
Integrate what is learned by using technology with what is learned offline.	Students synthesize the information learned through offline sources (video, cartoon, article, ABC list, analysis questions, mapping) with information learned through online research.
Select and use those [tools] best suited for communication.	Students represent what they learned through a print Bulletin Board Display or Digital Storytelling and write an essay to communicate what they have learned.

Guiding Student Development: Skills and Strategies

Let's consider some of the ways to guide students as they work toward independence with each of the skills needed for this literacy capacity.

Tailor searches online to acquire useful information efficiently

Even though our students are digital natives (to borrow a familiar phrase) and can use technology quite adeptly, they still may not know how to thoughtfully and critically conduct online research and use websites that are credible and useful for the purpose of particular assignments. The following are some specific strategies to pass on that will help students tailor their online searches to acquire useful information more efficiently.

ABCs

One way for students to consider whether they are searching for information that is useful is to have them consider the ABCs of searching:

A—Author: Is the author or publisher of the site reliable? What makes the author or site publisher an expert on this topic?

B—Bias: Are there any signs of bias? Are multiple perspectives addressed?

C—Credibility: Are the claims made credible? Is the evidence to support these claims sufficient?

ABCs is a useful mnemonic for evaluating both print and online sources. When students remember the ABCs of evaluating a source, they are more likely to consider its validity and reliability.

Differentiation highlights/tips: An ABCs-powered source evaluation can be conducted in pairs or small groups to provide additional support for struggling students or to model good responses. You can break down this activity even further by providing more specific questions about each letter. For example, questions about the author might include the following: What do you know about the author—what is his or her background, knowledge, and experience? How do you know this? Where did you get this information? Name three things that would make this author an expert in his or her field. Explain.

Two Truths and a Lie

Two Truths and a Lie is a fun parlor game you might have played at a party. Participants share two true statements about themselves and one lie, and members of their group have to guess which statements are true and which is the lie. The Two Truths and a Lie instructional strategy has students adapt this to source evaluation. Challenge students to find two sources that they think are reliable and one source that is not reliable. Have them share their selections in small groups, explain their reasoning (with reference to evidence), and see if their peers agree with their designations.

Differentiation highlights/tips: Any activity that gives ELLs a chance to practice their verbal skills is beneficial, but Two Truths and a Lie is also a great tool for creating a community of learners, and it gives you information you can use to tailor instruction to student interest as students share information about themselves and learn about one another. You can provide examples and model the activity to give them an idea of the kind of information that's appropriate to share. For example, Vicky posed these three statements to her students as an icebreaking activity on the first day of her course in the fall of 2015:

1. I am a former college soccer player.
2. I am terrified of roller coasters.
3. I enjoy watching apocalyptic zombie movies.

Can you guess which statement is the lie? Not so apparent, is it? Ninety percent of Vicky's students guessed incorrectly, and this led to a discussion of Vicky's avid enjoyment of soccer. Even though she never played the sport, all three of her children play, and her husband coaches their teams. Students shared which sports they enjoy and play, what teams they follow, and how much they like or dislike roller coasters and zombie movies. Both professor and students learned about each other, recognized and appreciated common interests and different likes, and bonded as a community of learners.

Five Ws, One H

The strategy Five Ws, One H gives students another mnemonic reminder to ask important questions about online sources they are examining:

• *Who* is the author of the site? What are the credentials of the author? Is there a Contact Us link? (Author)

• *What* is the relevance of the site to your topic? What information is presented? (Content)

• *Why* does the site exist? What is the purpose of the site? (Purpose)

• *Where* does the information come from? (.org, .com, .net, .gov)? Where can you find information on the site? What are other links? Where do these links take you? (Source and links)

• *When* was the site last updated? Is it recent? (Date)

• *How* is the information presented on the site? Is it well organized? Is it reader-friendly? Does the site have lots of pop-ups and advertisements? (Presentation)

Differentiation highlights/tips: Five Ws, One H is a strategy that all students can remember easily, especially if they use it when reading or writing informational texts. The focus questions help guide students' responses as they examine and evaluate a source. You can have students work in groups, each examining a W or H in multiple sources and becoming an expert in that area.

Integrate what is learned online with what is learned offline

In today's classrooms, which combine traditional means of instruction with new, technology-infused approaches, it's important that students understand how to learn expertly through both online and offline means. Here are some instructional strategies that will foster that understanding.

Thumball

Thumball was originally designed to be an icebreaker at parties. Available in many versions from many manufacturers, a Thumball is a soft, often colorful, miniature soccer ball that has words, numbers, or phrases printed in each square. The version we recommend using as a tool for activating students' prior knowledge before a lesson and checking in on their learning at the lesson's end features a letter in each square. You begin the activity by tossing the ball to a student volunteer. The student catches the ball, looks at the letter square his or her right thumb is touching, and then says a word beginning with that letter that is related to the topic at hand. In a lesson on global warming, for example, the student might say, "*C* for *climate change*." If no word comes to mind, the student has a fallback: the letter under his or her left thumb. You can use this tool for purposes beyond activating prior knowledge. For instance, as the students pass the ball back and forth, collect the terms they generate in a master list.

After everyone has touched the Thumball once and offered a topic, students consult the master list and go online to conduct research on a topic of their choosing. They find information about the topic, organize that information into a list of alphabetically ordered terms (e.g., *A* is for *Arctic sea ice*, *B* is for *biosphere*, *C* is for *carbon cycle*), and then report out to the rest of the class. The lesson ends with another round of Thumball to reinforce what students learned both by listening to one another and by conducting an online search.

Differentiation highlights/tips: This activity replaces a typical question-and-answer session with something out of the ordinary and kinesthetic. Instead of buying a "real" Thumball, you can create one of your own with a doctored soccer ball; this has the added benefit of making it easy to alter the activity. You might, for example, set up a ball featuring questions for students to respond to (and then research) or literary devices that they need to identify in a work they have read (and then research and document). You can also vary the rules of the game to increase or reduce challenge. For example, students who get stuck on a letter might say "Pass" no more than two times per round, or they might have the option to elicit help from their classmates.

Evidence Scavenger Hunt

This activity sends students on a quest to find information offline and online. It begins with you distributing a list of questions pertaining to a print text (literary or informational). These questions could refer to the text's content or structure (e.g., "What is the setting of the novel *To Kill a Mockingbird*?" "When do we celebrate Earth Day?"). After responding—individually, in pairs, or in small groups—students proceed to a curated list of websites where they can find answers to the same questions. They check their answers against what they find online, gather supporting evidence, and cite the sources in a specified format (e.g., Chicago, MLA). You can turn this into a race so that the student, pair, or team that finishes first with all the correct responses wins.

Differentiation highlights/tips: The grouping options in this activity allow you to set it up to suit different learning styles, and you might assign or allow students to choose their roles: scavenger, reader, note taker, and so on. You can provide scaffolding by naming the section of a website where an answer appears or by giving some students or teams a head start. You can vary the challenge by assigning fewer websites or more, or choosing websites with text that is more or less complex.

Bulletin Board Display

This strategy has students synthesize information about a complex topic gathered from print and online sources and present the information as a visual and textual display on a bulletin board (or sheet of poster board). Working in groups, students explore subtopics, carry out specific roles, and demonstrate their learning by identifying and combining essential and relevant content. For example, when studying the Vietnam War, groups might research descriptions of the war, the time period and historical context, causes, effects, American perspectives, Vietnamese perspectives, literature of the time, music of the time, and movie titles about the war. Determine in advance the number and type of sources that you want members to incorporate and the roles you'll have them assume in their groups, such as researcher, reliability investigator, reader, note taker, and bulletin board layout artist. The layout artist may seem at first like an easy choice, but it can be challenging because this student has to decide how to synthesize and represent all the information in a coherent and visually appealing way. Each group has a section of the board on which to display their work. The final product is an informative mosaic of a complex topic's various aspects.

Differentiation highlights/tips: In the Bulletin Board Display strategy, you can compose groups and assign roles depending on students' strengths, interests, or abilities—or you can allow students to choose roles themselves. You can adjust the challenge by varying topic options and the number and type of sources group members need to incorporate.

Select and use the tools best suited for communication

Students nowadays have myriad communication tools to choose from—most of them digital. Among others, there are tools for gathering and sharing information, for storytelling, and for social networking. A significant part of teaching students to select and use the tools best suited for particular kinds of communication is to expose them to various tools and explicitly call their attention to how each tool's capabilities support various communication purposes. The American Association of School Librarians (2013) has suggested the following tools, available at press time, as the ones best suited for the following types of communication.

Gathering and Sharing Information

Padlet allows students to post things on a virtual wall and collaborate with others using a unique URL. Students can work together on projects or share their work once it's complete. You might also use Padlet when employing the Bulletin Board Display strategy.

Smore helps students design and create flyers and newsletters. They can choose from an array of templates and colors and also add visuals, audio, and video. This is a fun way for students to create professional-looking handouts for conveying information and making announcements.

Digital Storytelling

FlipSnack is an app for converting PDF files to flipbooks. Students can turn reports or creative writing into flipbooks and also add color and graphics. The books look professional and can be shared with others electronically. Photo Story is a digital app that allows students to narrate a story using visual, audio, and video formats. Microsoft offers a free version of Photo Story for student use. The end result looks like a Ken Burns documentary.

Social Networking

BiblioNasium is a social network students can use to set up virtual bookshelves and communicate about their reading interests. They can share their favorite books with others. LitPick gives students access to free electronic books and promotes networking about books. Students write reviews for other students and post them anonymously. They can also participate in discussions with authors, publishers, and parents.

Differentiation highlights/tips: The digital tools that we suggest for gathering and sharing information, narrating stories, and networking with others support differentiation of content, process, and product for all learners. You, or your students, can choose tools that complement students' learning styles.

Test Connection

Figure 7.1 shows the CLI skill components featured in this chapter's Smarter Balanced test excerpt, how that task is assessing each component, and the teaching strategies we recommend to help students build the associated skills. Take a moment to identify the CLI components that are strengths for your students and those that are areas for improvement.

FIGURE 7.1

Using Technology and Digital Media: Skill Components, Demands of the Test, and Teaching Strategies

CLI Skill Components	Demands of the Test	Teaching Strategies
Tailor searches online to acquire useful information efficiently.	The task includes a list of Internet sources for students to read, evaluate, and cite as appropriate to the task.	ABCs Two Truths and a Lie Five Ws and One H
Integrate what is learned by using technology with what is learned offline.	Students may integrate what they know about the topic with the information presented in the source.	Thumball Evidence Scavenger Hunt Bulletin Board Display
Select and use those [tools] best suited for communication.	Students are required to use a word processing program.	Gathering and Sharing Information Digital Storytelling Social Networking

Stage 3 Reflection

What activities, instruction, sources, and methods would promote your students' understanding, interest, and excellence in this literacy capacity? How do the lessons you use now and the strategies you currently employ to help your students use technology and visual media parallel the instructional procedures presented in this chapter? What changes might you make?

When we think about next generation assessment, the changes related to technology stand out. For so many of our students, technology plays a central role in their day-to-day lives. As teachers, there is a lot we can do to support students' strategic use of technology.

One of the many benefits of technology is the way that it connects us. Students can use it to communicate with and learn about people with views and experiences that are vastly different from their own. In this way, it helps them come to understand other perspectives and cultures, the capacity addressed in the next chapter.

8

Understanding Other Perspectives and Cultures

Students appreciate that the 21st century classroom and workplace are settings in which people from often widely divergent cultures and who represent diverse experiences and perspectives must learn and work together. Students actively seek to understand other perspectives and cultures through reading and listening, and they are able to communicate effectively with people of varied backgrounds. They evaluate other points of view critically and constructively. Through reading great classic and contemporary works of literature representative of a variety of periods, cultures, and worldviews, students can vicariously inhabit worlds and have experiences much different than their own. (CCSSI, 2015)

In this chapter, we turn to ways to help students gain or further their understanding of other perspectives and cultures.

It's a timely focus for a highly connected age. Today's technology allows us to network and form relationships with people all over the world via the Internet, Twitter, Facebook, Instagram, Skype, and other platforms. Schools are becoming more and more diverse, filled with young people who have different cultural and linguistic backgrounds and different life experiences. To work well together, our students need to develop cultural consciousness and effective communication skills. They need the ability to appraise perspectives that they may not necessarily share and to develop respect for these different cultures.

We should note that the term *culture,* as we're using it here, is an expansive one, meant to extend beyond the traditional definition of customs and mores that are rooted in national origin. Yes, it's important to build understandings between students who grow up speaking different languages, but it's also important to ask what students understand about people who live in economic circumstances different from their own, what kind of understanding the stereotypical "nerd" has of the stereotypical "jock," what the heterosexual student understands about the LGBTQ student, and so on.

Both in our professional experiences and in our personal lives as mothers raising children, we have found that when young people are asked to consider alternative perspectives to their own, they have a hard time doing so. Why is this? We know from our preservice psychology training that children are egocentric, and that the ability to distinguish the objective from the subjective is part of cognitive development. The students in middle and high school classrooms are in the process of forming their own identities, which is an important aspect of growing up. As Erik Erikson (1963, 1968) reminds us, youngsters with a poor sense of self can struggle to relate to others and to form relationships. It is important for teachers to guide students as they develop into their identities and become more aware of their own and others' perspectives.

Let's begin our look at methods and strategies that can help even inwardly focused adolescents come to understand other perspectives and cultures. Remember, the description of the literate individual is where we want students to be upon graduation. Once again, we use the three stages of the backward design model (Desired Results, Evidence, and Instructional Procedures) to focus our inquiry and structure our planning.

Stage 1: Desired Results

We looked over the description of this CLI and found two key descriptors. To *understand other perspectives and cultures*, students must be able to

1. Actively seek to understand other perspectives and cultures through reading and listening.
2. Communicate effectively.

Stage 1 Reflection

Are you deliberately pursuing these outcomes in your instruction now? Pick out a few lessons that have these skills among the objectives and reflect on the methods and strategies that you are using to promote students' development of these skills. Are there other skills you see as essential to coming to understand other perspectives and cultures?

Stage 2: Evidence

Now we need to consider what it looks like to master the skills that constitute this CLI. The SAT question that follows is designed to measure students' ability to understand other perspectives and cultures. Note the interesting way that the College Board approaches this assessment objective: by asking students to consider cultural perspectives that span hundreds of years as well as international borders. Students must read and respond to selections from historical documents (e.g., the U.S. Constitution, the Bill of Rights, and the Federalist Papers) and texts that are part of "the Great Global Conversation," addressing issues of "freedom, justice, and human dignity" and how "we the people ought to live together in civil society" (College Board, 2014c, p. 1). The sample item we reproduce here does not include the text passage associated with it, but all texts are included in the actual test, and students can find the information they need to respond in the excerpts provided. These items do not assume prior knowledge of the texts in question.

SAMPLE TEST ITEMS

SAT Items Addressing the Great Global Conversation

Following is a text passage about the art and recreation of indigenous people in the American Southeast.

The main purpose of the passage is to

A. show how bizarre certain Southeastern Indian ceremonies and rituals are.
B. explain rules of several games played by Southeastern Indians.
C. describe the difficulties inherent in appreciating the Southeastern Indians' artistic and recreational forms.
D. explore the mysticism of the ceremonies and rituals in the Southeastern Indians' belief system.
E. delineate the difference between the artistic forms of the Southeastern Indians and the Cherokee Indians.

The author mentions the loss of many of the Indians' artistic and architectural creations (lines 19–20) in order to

A. criticize Indians' choice of materials.
B. provide an explanation for a problem.
C. underscore De Soto's appreciation for Indian creations.
D. delineate an impressive course of events.
E. anticipate a possible objection to a theory.

Source: Robinson & Katzman, 2014, p. 580.

Let's look at how the demands of the test relate to under-standing other perspectives and cultures as described in this CLI.

Demands of the Test	CLI Skill Components
Students seek to understand the Southeastern Indian culture through reading the passage.	Actively seek to understand other perspectives and cultures through reading and listening.
Students analyze the rhetorical choices that the writer makes in terms of mentioning the loss of many of the Indians' artistic and architectural creations (lines 19–20).	Communicate effectively.

Students must look at both the form and content of the passage in order to comprehend the information and ideas the writer presents and how the writer has chosen to construct the text.

Stage 2 Reflection

Is this assessment approach one that you use in your classroom? How do you gauge the progress students are making in their ability to understand other perspectives and cultures? How do you ask them to reflect upon and assess their own learning?

Stage 3: Instructional Procedures

Young people who are encouraged by parents, teachers, and peers to be successful are more likely to develop a strong sense of identity and belief in their abilities, and they are more likely to interact with others in positive ways. Therefore, we need to engage them in activities that involve self-exploration as well as an examination of diversity in terms of people's backgrounds, opinions, attitudes, points of view, ways of living, traditions and norms, relationships, languages, and so on. The following sample lesson scenario offers students multiple opportunities to further their identity development and to understand other perspectives and cultures.

SAMPLE LESSON SCENARIO
Examining and Expanding Students' Perspectives

Vicky's class began a unit on immigration. In order to activate her students' background knowledge and stimulate discussion, she distributed an Anticipation Guide (see p. 123) that contained a list of statements about immigration; students had to note if they agreed or disagreed with each statement. Vicky then led the class through a presentation that showed the correct answers, pausing after every three slides so that students could do a Turn and Talk (see p. 128). At the end of this activity, students reviewed their Anticipation Guide responses and revised the incorrect statements with accurate information from the presentation.

The next assignment involved students responding to various poems about immigration, noting personal reflections and new insights they had developed through reading them. The students

SAMPLE LESSON SCENARIO (*continued*)
Examining and Expanding Students' Perspectives

who were immigrants themselves or who had relatives who were immigrants had the opportunity to share their experiences of coming to the United States. Vicky led a class discussion about what it is like to migrate to a different country, guiding students to the understanding that even those who have not had the experience firsthand can relate to the feeling of being an outsider. This opened the door to rich conversations about what it is like to try to belong and be a part of a group, a culture, or a community but not fit in.

Having laid this foundation, Vicky saw her students were ready to read and respond to chapters from a story posted on In Our Global Village (www.inourvillage.org/IOGV). This website, facilitated by the organization What Kids Can Do, gives young people throughout the world a chance to share stories about their lives and learn about the lives of others. Vicky announced to her students they would be adding the story of their community to this website.

The first step was to examine the model story. Vicky structured this activity as a Collaborative Cafe (see pp. 126–127), and students worked in groups to determine their chapter's main ideas, share these ideas with other groups, and finally represent the information in a mind map or concept web. Next, students conducted a closer reading of their assigned chapter and analyzed how the style and structure supported its content. With this model in mind, students worked in groups to write their own In Our Global Village chapters to tell the story of their community. All group members (Vicky set up six groups, with four members in each) participated in selecting the topic and writing about it in an essay. Each member also had an additional role: photography, layout, editing, or quote seeking. The topics students could select from included their community's school, language, food, religion, architecture (houses/buildings/stores), and clubs. Vicky wrote the first chapter about the history of the community. Students revised and polished their chapters after receiving teacher and classmate feedback. At the lesson's end, the chapters were compiled in a flipbook and published on the In Our Global Village website.

Connecting the Lesson with the CLI

Let's look at this lesson through the lens of the target CLI—*understand other perspectives and cultures:*

CLI Skill Components	Lesson Components
Actively seek to understand other perspectives and cultures through reading and listening.	Students respond to immigration Anticipation Guide and poems. They read and analyze an In Our Global Village story.
Communicate effectively.	Students write their own stories.
	Students share their stories with the class/school and publish them online for a global audience.

Guiding Students' Development: Skills and Strategies

Now it's time to consider ways to guide students as they work toward independence with each of the skills needed for this capacity.

Actively seek to understand other perspectives and cultures through reading and listening

As we noted earlier, sometimes students struggle to envision or understand perspectives other than their own. Finding a common element is often the key that will open their eyes to what others are thinking or feeling. In the case of Vicky's immigration lesson, all students had experienced the feeling of "being other." This could also apply to how an LGBTQ student might feel in a classroom or to the way a struggling student might feel when involved in cooperative learning. It is extremely important to get students thinking about their own preconceptions and consulting reliable information that they can use to reinforce, refine, or revise these preconceptions over time.

The following strategies enable students to strengthen their ability to understand other perspectives and cultures through reading and listening.

Anticipation Guide

The Anticipation Guide strategy is employed to activate students' prior knowledge and stimulate their interest before they read, view, or listen to a text. It involves distributing a prepared list of statements and asking students to agree or disagree with each statement in writing and explain each response (see Figure 8.1). The point is not for students to "answer correctly" but to think about what they know and believe about a topic they will soon study. After students read, view, or listen to the text, they revisit their responses, confirm or refine them, and make necessary changes.

FIGURE 8.1

Anticipation Guide

Anticipation Guide—Immigration

Directions: Read each statement and agree or disagree with it. Explain your response in the space provided. After viewing the presentation, revisit your responses and revise them if necessary.

Statements	Before the Presentation	After the Presentation
1. Immigrants in the U.S. create jobs as consumers and entrepreneurs.	I agree/disagree because . . .	I agree/disagree because . . .
2. Many successful Americans are immigrants.	I agree/disagree because . . .	I agree/disagree because . . .
3. The first significant federal legislation restricting immigration was the 1882 Chinese Exclusion Act.	I agree/disagree because . . .	I agree/disagree because . . .
4. Immigrants came through Ellis Island, the country's first federal immigration station.	I agree/disagree because . . .	I agree/disagree because . . .
5. A teenager from County Cork, Ireland, was the first immigrant processed at Ellis Island.	I agree/disagree because . . .	I agree/disagree because . . .
6. Most people came to America seeking asylum.	I agree/disagree because . . .	I agree/disagree because . . .
7. In 1985, Congress passed the Immigration and Nationality Act, which did away with quotas.	I agree/disagree because . . .	I agree/disagree because . . .
8. Today, the majority of U.S. immigrants come from Europe.	I agree/disagree because . . .	I agree/disagree because . . .

For information about immigration, go to
http://www.pewresearch.org/fact-tank/2015/11/19/5-facts-about-illegal-immigration-in-the-u-s/
http://www.history.com/topics/u-s-immigration-before-1965
http://www.history.com/topics/us-immigration-since-1965
http://www.immigrationpolicy.org/just-facts

Duffelmeyer (1994) highlights the steps to take when preparing and using an Anticipation Guide:

1. Identify the major ideas presented in the text.

2. Consider the beliefs your students are likely to have about the topic addressed.

3. Write general statements that are likely to challenge your students' beliefs.

4. Require students to respond to the statements with either a positive or negative response.

Differentiation highlights/tips: The Anticipation Guide is an effective strategy because it invites all students to share their perspectives and does not assume prior knowledge. It also stimulates students' thinking about a topic—what they know or may not know. You can gauge and build on this knowledge even as you address knowledge gaps. This is another strategy with a format that allows for several means of differentiation. You can vary the statements you provide to address your instructional purpose, to target basic to higher-level thinking, and to manage the level of challenge or controversy appropriate for the particular lesson and your students. You can also use students' names in the statements or write statements that revolve around their interests, which can be extremely motivating and validating for your diverse students.

Mirrors/Windows

This strategy was created by a colleague, David Smith, to stimulate reflection and new insights on a topic that students encounter in written, spoken, or visual texts. You can give students a prepared handout with or without sentence starters (see Figure 8.2) or have them take out a piece of paper, fold it in half, and set up a table themselves. The column on the left is labeled "Mirrors," and like mirrors, it's about reflection. Here students record personal reflections on the topic. In the "Windows" column on the right, they record new insights and realizations—as if they were looking outside a window at a new scene.

FIGURE 8.2
Mirrors/Windows Organizer

Mirrors	Windows
I know _____ about this topic. This reminds me of . . . This makes me think of . . .	I learned . . . A new insight or idea that I have as a result of this text is . . .

Differentiation highlights/tips: Mirrors/Windows is a strategy where all students can think on paper and record their feelings, ideas, and opinions. The concept windows and mirrors will help students remember what they need to do as well as what they wrote on their chart. Note, too, that the inward-looking, reflective slant of this strategy encourages personal connection, which tends to increase student engagement.

Pause, Write, COMPEL

The Pause, Write, COMPEL strategy can be used throughout the reading process to make comprehension more manageable. Students read a portion of the text, pause, and then write their thoughts—in the margins, below the text, or on a separate piece of paper. To make it more structured so that students concentrate on specific elements (as Vicky did during her students' analysis of the In Our Global Village story), you need to prepare focus questions that will COMPEL (it's an acronym) a thoughtful engagement with the text. Here is an example:

> Read one paragraph at a time from the Language chapter of the story "Boyle Heights Through the Eyes of Its Youth." On a separate piece of paper, label the paragraph by number and respond to the following five COMPEL questions:
>
> 1. Write one personal CONNECTION to this paragraph (feeling, emotion, association, memory, text-to-text links, or text-to-world links). For example: *This can be related to my situation because I am bilingual and also enjoy learning new languages.*

2. Write your **O**PINION of this paragraph. For example: *In my opinion, language is essential to a person's identity.*
3. Write what the paragraph is about (**M**AIN IDEA). For example:
   *This paragraph is about how language shapes the community of
   Boyle Heights.*
4. Write the author's message or **P**ERSPECTIVE on the topic. For
   example: *In this paragraph, the author wants to convey how
   important different languages are in the community and how
   much the people appreciate them.*
5. Write the **E**VIDENCE and **L**ANGUAGE (words, lines, literary elements, or rhetorical devices—repetition, metaphor, alliteration,
   etc.) that support the author's message. For example: *"Hello"
   or "Hola"; "enjoy learning new words"; "shapes our community";
   "vibrant mixture of languages."*

Differentiation highlights/tips: Pause, Write, COMPEL familiarizes
students with a staged, consistent process for reflection. You
can assign your more advanced students to read and respond to
bigger chunks of text and your struggling learners to read smaller
chunks, like phrases or sentences. The types of questions can
vary from basic to very challenging.

Communicate effectively

Students often need guidance in making choices about what
information to share, how to speak with others in a clear and
concise manner, and how best to organize information while
speaking or writing. The follow strategies guide students in their
development as effective communicators.

Collaborative Café

In Collaborative Café, students participate in a multilayered,
Jigsaw-style activity that engages them in reading, writing, listening, speaking, graphically representing, and viewing. It asks
students to make decisions, gather important information, draw
their own conclusions, and communicate varied ideas to one
another. There are four basic steps:

1. *Reading and summarizing.* Working in groups, each of which will examine one aspect of the topic being studied, students read their group's assigned text and collaborate to list three important facts it contains on a summary notes page. Students within a group may read silently or take turns reading aloud, but they must discuss the text together and make sure everyone in the group understands it.

2. *Note sharing.* Students walk around the room and listen to individuals from the other groups read the summary points of the texts that they read. The listeners add these summary notes to their own summary notes pages.

3. *Notes discussion.* Students return to their original group to discuss the information they have gathered and how the various pieces fit together to form a complex view of the topic.

4. *Mind mapping.* Each group develops a mind map or web that represents the most important information regarding all the topics that were explored.

Differentiation highlights/tips: This strategy offers many ways to ensure that all students are successfully working and engaging with text. You can differentiate the readings by carefully selecting levels and topics that are appropriate for your learners. If students are unfamiliar with key words, you can prompt them to use context clues to figure out the meaning or look them up in the dictionary; alternatively, you can provide a list of vocabulary words and their definitions. Note taking can be made more manageable by varying the number of summary points required. The visual representation in the form of a mind map or concept web allows students the flexibility to decide what is important to represent on paper. To provide more structure to the mapping process, you can assign roles: an organizer to take charge of the connections, a layout artist (perhaps an artistic student or one with strong spatial intelligence) to create and place artwork and illustrations, a documentarian (a student with good penmanship and note-taking skills) to transfer notes to the chart paper, and a presenter (a student with strong oral communication skills) to take the lead on the report-out.

Turn and Talk

Turn and Talk allows all students to participate in meaningful discussion. Although the way this strategy is used varies, it employs three basic steps:

1. *Question.* Pose a question that you want students to discuss. It could be a question about an old topic that you want to review or a new topic that you want to introduce.

2. *Turn.* Students turn to talk to an assigned partner. Partners should change periodically so that students have the opportunity to discuss their ideas with other classmates.

3. *Talk.* Students talk to their partners about the topic. Make sure you give students a time frame (e.g., two minutes) so they know how much time they have to engage in a discussion. You may want to make this step more structured so that students know *how* to talk. Prompts, like those in Figure 8.3—distributed or posted in the classroom—might be useful.

FIGURE 8.3
Turn and Talk Prompts and Scaffolds

When It's Your Turn . . .
Ask yourself: *What do I think about the topic?* State your answer clearly in one or two sentences. Ask yourself: *Why do I think this? How do I explain it? What evidence supports my opinion?* Give one or two examples from your prior knowledge or experiences.

When It's Your Partner's Turn . . .
Ask your partner: *What do you think about this topic, and why?* Allow two minutes for a response. If your partner is struggling to express an opinion or provide supporting evidence, ask questions and provide encouragement. Try these: *So, what opinions have you heard about this topic? Do you agree with any of those? Can you tell me more? What makes you think this way—personal experiences, background, interactions or conversations with teachers/peers/parents/relatives/friends, print or online readings, previous coursework?*

When It's Your Turn Again . . .
Respond to your partner's comments. Here are some ways to start your response: *I agree with you because . . . I disagree because . . . I had a similar experience . . . This makes me think of . . . This makes me have a question about . . .*

When It's Your Partner's Turn Again . . .
Your partner offers a concluding statement. Ask yourself: *How would I sum up the conversation and both our opinions? Any similarities? Any differences?*

Differentiation highlights/tips: Turn and Talk, with its predictable structure and scaffolded discussion points, gives all students opportunities to communicate with their peers in constructive ways. This strategy is especially beneficial for less vocal or more reticent students; speaking to a partner is often less intimidating than speaking in a whole-group setting. You can pair more advanced ELLs with beginning ELLs or nonnative speakers with native speakers.

Writing Frames

Writing Frames are like training wheels that benefit all learners who might know what they want to say but need the linguistic or organizational support to express it. As students develop their writing skills, you should remove these training wheels so that they can develop their own style and become more independent writers. See Figure 8.4 for an example of a Writing Frame for an informative/narrative essay that could be published as part of an In Our Global Village story like the one Vicky's students created.

Differentiation highlights/tips: Writing Frames provide an organizational structure for all students as well as linguistic support for your ELLs. You can include as much information and scaffolding as needed, depending on the diversity of your students (e.g., directions, tasks, expectations, sentence or word starters, transition words, various sentence types, etc.). You can give a blank frame to advanced students, challenging them to be their own guides, or a frame with visuals or even a word bank to your ELLs.

Test Connection

Let's look back at the sample SAT items presented on page 119. Figure 8.5 outlines the CLI skill components it is assessing, the construct that is measuring each component, and teaching strategies that may help prepare students for success with each component.

FIGURE 8.4
Writing Frame

Paragraph 1: Introduction
Craft a catchy first sentence.

While walking down the streets of Long Island City, one can (see, hear, taste, smell, or feel)

_____

_____

Tell what a person might see, hear, taste, smell, or feel in relation to your topic.

_____

_____

Paragraphs 2 and 3: Development
Describe the topic/sensory experience related to the topic. Provide two or three examples of figurative language. Choose your words wisely so that they accurately express what you want to say.

_____ has left a mark on the community.

One can see _____.

One can hear _____.

One can feel _____.

It is like _____.

For example, _____.

As a result, _____.

Paragraph 4: Significance
Discuss the significance of the topic. Why is it important to the community? What are its effects on the community? What are its benefits?

_____ is important to the community because _____

_____.

Paragraph 5: Conclusion
What is the importance of the topic in a broader sense? What can we conclude about it?

We can conclude that _____

_____.

FIGURE 8.5

Understanding Other Perspectives and Cultures: Skill Components, Demands of the Test, and Teaching Strategies

CLI Components	Demands of the Test	Teaching Strateiges
Actively seek to understand other perspectives and cultures through reading and listening.	Students read the passage to develop an understanding of South-eastern Indian culture.	Anticipation Guide Mirrors/Windows Pause, Write, COMPEL
Communicate effectively.	Students analyze the rhetorical choices that the writer makes in terms of mentioning the loss of many of the Indians' artistic and architectural creations (lines 19–20).	Collaborative Café Turn and Talk Writing Frames

Stage 3 Reflection

What activities, instruction, sources, and methods would promote your students' understanding, interest, and excellence in this literacy capacity? How do the lessons you use now and the strategies you currently employ to help your students understand other perspectives and cultures parallel the instructional procedures presented in this chapter? What changes might you make?

In a world that is getting smaller thanks to technology, travel accessibility, and jobs that take us far from home, the ability to understand other perspectives and communicate effectively with diverse populations is ever more important. As we help students develop this literacy capacity, we must continuously consider how to help them use their abilities to become model global citizens who are respectful of peers across the classroom and around the world.

Conclusion: Fostering Independence with Carefully Chosen Strategies

---

Throughout this text, we have discussed effective strategies for guiding secondary students' literacy development. We have advocated consulting various next generation test items in order to examine their demands, because doing so clarifies how next generation literacy is being defined and measured. And in each of the chapters in Part II, we have focused on how to go about developing six of the seven capacities of the literate individual, as defined in the Common Core Standards for English Language Arts and Literacy.

As we mentioned in the Introduction, we were mindful in leaving out the first capacity because we see it as a broad overview of the independence that we want students to develop as literate individuals by the time they graduate from high school:

Students can, without significant scaffolding, comprehend and evaluate complex texts across a range of types and disciplines, and they can construct effective arguments and convey intricate or multifaceted information. Likewise, students are able independently to discern a speaker's key points, request clarification, and ask relevant questions. They build on others' ideas, articulate their own ideas, and confirm they have been understood. Without prompting, they demonstrate command of standard English and acquire and use a wide-ranging vocabulary. More broadly, they become self-directed learners, effectively seeking out and using resources to assist them, including teachers, peers, and print and digital reference materials. (CCSSI, 2015)

This first capacity lists so many ways that we want students to be independent in their reading, writing, speaking, and language use. The six capacities discussed at some length in Part II support these varied types of independence. Of course, we realize that the capacities overlap throughout the chapters, but we categorized the lessons by what we viewed as the most prominent capacities.

Now take a moment to consider your students. With which capacities are they exhibiting progress toward independence? With which capacities are they struggling? How do you know? What teaching strategies might you use to foster their mastery and independence?

Aligning Strategies with the Capacities

To help you quickly and easily find strategies that will promote particular aspects of next generation literacy, we present the master chart on pages 135–136. Think of it as an à la carte menu to consult when designing lessons to address a particular CLI—or multiple CLI. Combine these 42 strategies in a way that suits your objectives and benefits your students.

Strategies for Developing the Capacities of the Literate Individual

Note: The ● symbol indicates the CLI associated with the strategy in this book; the ○ symbol indicates other CLI that the strategy might be used to develop.

Strategy	Build Strong Content Knowledge	Respond to Audience, Task, Purpose, and Discipline	Comprehend as well as Critique	Value Evidence	Use Technology and Digital Media	Understand Other Perspectives and Cultures
ABCs	○	○	○	○	●	○
Advertising Analysis		●	○	○	○	○
Annotation	●		○	○		
Anticipation Guide	○	○		○		●
Blackout Poetry	○	○	○	●		○
Bulletin Board Display	○	○	○	○	●	○
Carousel Analysis	○	○	○	●		○
Collaborative Café	○	○	○	○		●
Debate	●	○	○	○		○
Developing a Flyer	●	○	○	○	○	○
Digital Storytelling	○	○	○	○	●	○
Directed Reading Thinking Activity (DRTA)	●		○	○		
Double-Sided Notes	●		○	○		
Evidence Scavenger Hunt	○	○	○	○	●	
Five Ws and One H	○	○	○	○	●	○
Four Square	●		○	○	○	○
Gathering and Sharing Information	○	○	○	○	●	○
Guided Notes	●		○	○	○	○
Guided Peer Response	○	○	●	○		○
ICE Your Quotes	○	○	○	●		○

Strategy	Build Strong Content Knowledge	Respond to Audience, Task, Purpose, and Discipline	Comprehend as well as Critique	Value Evidence	Use Technology and Digital Media	Understand Other Perspectives and Cultures
Improvised Debate		○	●	○		
Interdisciplinary Thinking Concept Map	○	●	○	○		○
Language Awareness		●	○	○		
Liar, Liar!	○	●	○	○		
Literary Analysis Essay Planner	○	○	○	●		
Literature Circles	○	○	○	●		○
MAAPP CEnteR	○	○	●	○		○
Mirrors/Windows	○	○	○			●
Pause, Write, COMPEL	○	○	○	○		●
Playing with Voice		●	○			○
Point of View Writing	○	○	●	○		○
Reflective Listening	●	○	○	○		○
Scaffolded Critique	○	○	●	○		○
Social Networking		○			●	○
Source Analysis	○	●	○	○		○
Source Analysis Graphic Organizer	○	○	○	●		
Think Aloud	○	○	●	○		○
Thumball	○			○	●	
Turn and Talk	○	○	○	○		●
Two Truths and a Lie				○	●	○
Writing a Proposal	●	○	○	○		○
Writing Frames	○	○	○	○		●

Taking Action

In the Introduction to this book, we stressed that our own "Stage 1: Desired Results" when we write together is always to share practical information with our colleagues. The evidence that we gather to assess whether or not we have produced a work that reflects this desired result is your feedback. Just as we want students to think beyond the test, we want you to think beyond your reading of this book. Make the 42 strategies within this book your own. Adapt them to fit your students' needs. Apply them to develop the capacities of the literate individual. Then, please, share your success stories with us.

References

ACT. (2009). *ACT national curriculum survey 2009.* Iowa City, IA: Author.

ACT. (2014a). *The condition of college and career readiness 2014: National.* Washington, DC: Author. Retrieved from http://www.act.org/content /act/en/research/condition-of-college-and-career-readiness-report-2014.html

ACT. (2014b). About the ACT test: Science test description. Retrieved from http://www.act.org/content/act/en/products-and-services/the-act-educator/about-the-act.html

ACT. (2015). About the ACT writing test: Writing test scores. Retrieved from http://www.act.org/content/act/en/products-and-services/the-act-educator/about-the-act/act-plus-writing.html

Alleyne, R. (2011, February 11). Welcome to the information age—174 newspapers a day. Retrieved from http://www.telegraph.co.uk/news/science/science-news/8316534/Welcome-to-the-information-age-174-newspapers-a-day.html

American Association of School Librarians. (2013). Best websites for teaching & learning 2013. Retrieved from http://www.ala.org/aasl/standards-guidelines/best-websites/2013

Applebee, A. N., & Langer, J. A. (2009). What is happening in the teaching of writing? *English Journal, 98*(5), 18–28.

College Board. (2014a). The redesigned SAT: Analysis in science and in history/social studies. Retrieved from https://www.collegereadi ness.collegeboard.org/pdf/analysis-science-history-social-studies .pdf

College Board. (2014b). The redesigned SAT: Essay analyzing a source. Retrieved from https://www.collegeboard.org/sites/default/files/essay_analyzing_a_source.pdf

College Board. (2014c). The redesigned SAT: Founding documents and the great global conversation. Retrieved from https://www.collegeboard.org/sites/default/files/founding_documents_and_the_great_global_conversation.pdf

College Board. (2014d). The redesigned SAT: Test specifications for the redesigned SAT. Retrieved from https://collegereadiness.collegeboard.org/pdf/test-specifications-redesigned-sat-1.pdf

College Board (2014e). Sample questions: Reading. Retrieved from https://collegereadiness.collegeboard.org/sample-questions/reading

College Board. (2015a). Compare SAT specifications. Retrieved from https://collegereadiness.collegeboard.org/sat/inside-the-test/compare-old-new-specifications

College Board. (2015b). Key content changes. Retrieved from https://collegereadiness.collegeboard.org/about/key-changes

College Board. (2015c). Sample questions: Essay. Retrieved from https://collegereadiness.collegeboard.org/sample-questions/essay/

Common Core State Standards Initiative. (2015). English language arts standards: Introduction: Students who are college and career ready in reading, writing, speaking, listening, & language. Retrieved from http://www.corestandards.org/ELA-Literacy/introduction/students-who-are-college-and-career-ready-in-reading-writing-speaking-listening-language/

Connolly, E., & Giouroukakis, V. (2011). Voices from the field: Technology and multimodal learning in a teacher education course. *The English Record, 61*(1), 2–11.

Duffelmeyer, F. (1994). Effective anticipation guide statements for learning from expository prose. *Journal of Reading, 37,* 452–455.

Dulan, S. W. (2012). *Conquering ACT English, reading, and writing* (2nd ed.). New York: McGraw-Hill.

Erikson, E. H. (1963). *Childhood and society* (2nd ed.). New York: Norton.

Erikson, E. H. (1968). *Identity: Youth and crisis.* New York: Norton.

Fadel, C. (2008). Multimodal learning through media: What the research says. Retrieved from http://www.cisco.com/c/dam/en_us/solutions/industries/docs/education/Multimodal-Learning-Through-Media.pdf

Florida Department of Education. (n.d.). Grade 9 FCAT 2.0 reading sample questions. Retrieved from http://www.fldoe.org/core/fileparse.php/3/urlt/fl540182_gr9rdgstm_tb_wt_r2g.pdf

Giouroukakis, V., & Connolly, M. (2012). *Getting to the core of English language arts, grades 6–12.* Thousand Oaks, CA: Corwin.

Giouroukakis, V., & Connolly, M. (2013). *Getting to the core of literacy in history/social studies, science, and technical subjects, grades 6–12.* Thousand Oaks, CA: Corwin.

Guilfoile, L., & Ryan, M. (2013). *Linking service-learning and the Common Core State Standards: Alignment, progress, and obstacles.* Denver, CO: Education Commission of the States. Retrieved from http://www.communityworksinstitute.org/cwpublications/ecs_common coreands-l.pdf

Halpern, D. F. (2001). Assessing the effectiveness of critical thinking instruction. *Journal of General Education, 50*(4), 270–286.

Hatch, L. Z., & Hatch, J. D. (2015). *ACT for dummies.* Hoboken, NJ: Wiley.

Hill, R. (2011). Common Core curriculum and complex texts. *Teacher Librarian, 38*(3), 42–46.

Karami, M., Pakmehr, H., & Aghili, A. (2012). Another view to importance of teaching methods in curriculum: Collaborative learning and students' critical thinking disposition. *Social and Behavioral Sciences, 46*, 3266–3270.

Kaye, C. B. (2010). *The complete guide to service learning.* Minneapolis, MN: Free Spirit.

Kerr, N. H., & Picciotti, M. (1992). Linked composition courses: Effects on student performance. *Journal of Teaching Writing, 11*(1), 105–118.

Lai, E. R. (2011). Critical thinking: A literature review [Research report]. Retrieved from http://images.pearsonassessments.com/images/tmrs/CriticalThinkingReviewFINAL.pdf

Marin, L. M., & Halpern, D. F. (2011). Pedagogy for developing critical thinking in adolescents: Explicit instruction produces greatest gains. *Thinking Skills and Creativity, 6*, 1–13.

Martz, G., Magliore, K., & Silver, T. (2014). *Cracking the ACT premium.* Natick, MA: Princeton Review.

Massachusetts Department of Secondary Education. (2013). Massachusetts Comprehensive Assessment System, 2013 spring release: VII. English language arts, reading comprehension, grade 8. Retrieved from http://www.doe.mass.edu/mcas/2013/release/g8ela.pdf

National Center for Education Statistics (2012). *The nation's report card: Writing 2011* (NCES 2012–470). Washington, DC: Institute of Education Sciences, U.S. Department of Education. Retrieved from http://nces.ed.gov/nationsreportcard/pdf/main2011/2012470.pdf

Partnership for Assessment of Readiness for College and Careers. (2013). Advances in the PARCC ELA/literacy summative assessment: Grade 9 sample end-of-year set. Retrieved from http://www.rvrhs.com/ourpages/auto/2015/1/15/61431418/Grade%209%20English%20Sample%20Items%20PPT.pdf

Partnership for Assessment of Readiness for College and Careers. (2014). Updated item guidelines for ELA/literacy PARCC summative assessment. Retrieved from http://www.jcboe.org/boe2015/images/ PARCCCCSS/Updated_Formatted_Item_Guidelines_pdf

Partnership for Assessment of Readiness for College and Careers. (2015a). Grade 8 ELA/literacy practice test. Retrieved from http:// epat-parcc.testnav.com/client/index.html#login?username=PT08E& password=Practice

Partnership for Assessment of Readiness for College and Careers. (2015b). Grade 10 ELA/literacy practice test. Retrieved from http:// epat-parcc.testnav.com/client/index.html#login?username=PT10E& password=Practice

Partnership for Assessment of Readiness for College and Careers. (2015c). Grade 11 ELA/literacy practice test. Retrieved from http:// parcc.pearson.com/resources/practice-tests/english/grade-11/pba/ PC194889-001_11ELATB_PT.pdf

Perie, M., Grigg, W. S., & Donahue, P. L. (2005). *The nation's report card: Reading 2005* (NCES 2006–451). U.S. Department of Education, Institute of Education Sciences, National Center for Education Statistics. Washington, DC: U.S. Government Printing Office.

Princeton Review. (2015). *10 practice tests for the SAT: For students taking the SAT in 2015 or January 2016.* New York: Author.

Purcell, K., Rainie, L., Heaps, A., Buchanan, J., Friedrich, L, Jacklin, A., Chen, C., & Zickuhr, K. (2012, November 1). How teens do research in the digital world. Retrieved from http://www.pewinternet .org/2012/11/01/how-teens-do-research-in-the-digital-world/

Robinson, A., & Katzman, J. (2014). *Cracking the SAT: Premium 2015 edition.* Natick, MA: Princeton Review.

Roell, K. C. (2012). *ACT strategy smart.* Piscataway, NJ: Research & Education Association.

Rosen, L. J., & Behrens, L. (Eds.). (1994). *The Allyn & Bacon handbook.* Boston: Allyn & Bacon.

Silver, D. (2014, December 22). Toy makers are listening to consumers about gender options. Retrieved from http://www.nytimes.com/ roomfordebate/2014/12/22/why-should-toys-come-in-pink-and-blue/ toy-makers-are-listening-to-consumers-about-gender-options

Smarter Balanced Assessment Consortium. (n.d.). Sample items and performance tasks. Retrieved December 6, 2015, from http://www .smarterbalanced.org/sample-items-and-performance-tasks/

Smarter Balanced Assessment Consortium. (2011). Appendix B: Grade level tables for all claims and assessment targets and item types. Retrieved December 6, 2015, from http://www.smarterbalanced .org/wordpress/wp-content/uploads/2011/12/ELA-Literacy-Content-Specifications.pdf

Smarter Balanced Assessment Consortium. (2012, April 16). General item specifications—Draft. Retrieved December 6, 2015, from http://www.smarterbalanced.org/wordpress/wp-content/uploads/2012/05/TaskItemSpecifications/ItemSpecifications/GeneralItem Specifications.pdf

Smarter Balanced Assessment Consortium. (2013, August 26). Practice test scoring guide—Grade 7. Retrieved from http://sbac.portal.airast.org/wp-content/uploads/2015/04/Grade7ELA.pdf

Smarter Balanced Assessment Consortium. (2014a, May 8). English/language arts CAT practice test scoring guide—Grade 8. Retrieved from http://sbac.portal.airast.org/wp-content/uploads/2013/08/G8_PracticeTest_ScoringGuide_ELA.pdf

Smarter Balanced Assessment Consortium. (2014b, May 16). English/language arts practice test scoring guide—Grade 11 performance task. Retrieved November 17, 2015, from http://www.smarterbalanced.org/wordpress/wp-content/uploads/2015/08/ELA_Practice_Test_Scoring_Guide_Grade_11_PT.pdf

Smarter Balanced Assessment Consortium. (2015a.). Sample items and performance tasks. Retrieved December 6, 2015 from http://www.smarterbalanced.org/sample-items-and-performance-tasks

Smarter Balanced Assessment Consortium. (2015b). Smarter Balanced assessments. Retrieved December 6, 2015 from http://www.smarterbalanced.org/smarter-balanced-assessments/

Tennessee Department of Education. (2015). TNReady sample items, English language arts. Retrieved from http://www.tncore.org/sites/www/Uploads/Leadership%20Resources/TNReady%20ELA%20Samples%20%289-12%29.pdf

Texas Education Agency. (2014). State of Texas Assessments of Academic Readiness: English I: Writing. Retrieved from http://www.tea.texas.gov/WorkArea/DownloadAsset.aspx?id=25769814926

University of the State of New York. (2015, January). Regents high school examination: Regents examination in English language arts (Common Core). Retrieved from http://www.nysedregents.org/hsela/115/hsela12015-exam.pdf

Wiggins, G., & McTighe, J. (2005). *Understanding by design* (Expanded 2nd ed.). Alexandria, VA: ASCD.

Index

Note: Page references followed by an italicized *f* indicate information contained in figures.

About the Authors

 **Maureen Connolly**, **EdD**, teaches undergraduate and graduate courses in secondary education for the School of Education at The College of New Jersey and is a consultant for CBK Associates. Before that, she was an English teacher at Mineola High School on Long Island, New York, for 15 years.

Maureen is the coauthor of the Corwin best-seller *Getting to the Core of English Language Arts, Grades 6–12: How to Meet the Common Core State Standards with Lessons from the Classroom,* and *Getting to the Core of Literacy for History/Social Studies, Science, and Technical Subjects, Grades 6–12.* She has overseen service learning grants for the New York metropolitan area and collaborated on several publications related to service learning. In these roles, she has developed many standards-based initiatives that link community outreach, character education, and literacy. Maureen was awarded the title of Honoree for the ASCD Outstanding Young

Educator of the Year and received the LEAD Award from St. John's University. She was selected by Teachers for the Global Classroom for an international fellowship in Morocco, and her international education experience also includes volunteering to teach in India, Ghana, Peru, and Spain.

Maureen believes that at the core of her profession is the need to develop purposeful learning that opens students' eyes to the potential for positive change in themselves and in their local, national, and global communities. She resides in New Jersey with her wonderful husband and two happy, smart, and kind children. Maureen can be reached at connollm@tcnj.edu.

Vicky Giouroukakis (née Menexas), **PhD**, is a professor in the Division of Education at Molloy College, Rockville Centre, New York. She teaches undergraduate and graduate courses in literacy, English education, and TESOL. Prior to her tenure at Molloy, Vicky taught English at a public high school in Queens, New York, and ESL to adolescents and adults.

Vicky is the coauthor of the Corwin best-seller *Getting to the Core of English Language Arts, Grades 6–12: How to Meet the Common Core State Standards with Lessons from the Classroom* and *Getting to the Core of Literacy for History/ Social Studies, Science, and Technical Subjects, Grades 6–12*. Her research and publications center on the topics of adolescent literacy, teacher education, cultural/linguistic diversity, and standards and assessment. She has been interested in standards and assessment and how they affect instructional practice ever since she began teaching. Vicky's work has been featured in books and scholarly journals, and she frequently presents at regional, national, and international conferences. She also serves as a consultant for the Boards of Cooperative Education Services

(BOCES) and provides professional development to various school districts.

Vicky received the Educator of Excellence Award from the New York State English Council in 2010 and the Research Achievement Award from Molloy College in 2015. She resides in New York with her supportive husband and three loving children and can be reached at vgiouroukakis@molloy.edu.

Related ASCD Resources:
Literacy, Standards, Assessment, and Lesson Design

At the time of publication, the following ASCD resources were available (ASCD stock numbers appear in parentheses). For up-to-date information about ASCD resources, go to www.ascd.org. You can search the complete archives of *Educational Leadership* at http://www.ascd.org/el.

Exchange ideas and connect with other educators on the social networking site ASCD EDge® at http://ascdedge.ascd.org/

Print Products

A Close Look at Close Reading: Teaching Students to Analyze Complex Texts, Grades 6–12 by Barbara Moss, Diane Lapp, Maria Grant, and Kelly Johnson (#115002)

Common Core State Standards for High School English Language Arts: A Quick-Start Guide by Susan Ryan and Dana Frazee; edited by John Kendall (#113010)

Common Core State Standards for Middle School English Language Arts: A Quick-Start Guide by Susan Ryan and Dana Frazee; edited by John Kendall (#113012)

Complex Text Decoded: How to Design Lessons and Use Strategies That Target Authentic Texts by Kathy T. Glass (#115006)

Teaching the Core Skills of Listening and Speaking by Erik Palmer (#114012)

Where Great Teaching Begins: Planning for Student Thinking and Learning by Anne R. Reeves (#111023)

PD Online®

Literacy: Language Arts and English (#PD09OC53M)

Literacy Strategies for Learning (#PD09OC52M)

Video

Assessment for 21st Century Learning: Transforming the 21st Century Learning Organization (DVD) (#610041)

Understanding by Design (DVD) (#600241)

THE WHOLE CHILD

ASCD's Whole Child approach is an effort to transition from a focus on narrowly defined academic achievement to one that promotes the long-term development and success of all children. Through this approach, ASCD supports educators, families, community members, and policymakers as they move from a vision about educating the whole child to sustainable, collaborative actions.

Achieving Next Generation Literacy: Using the Tests (You Think) You Hate to Help the Students You Love relates to the **challenged** tenet.

WHOLE CHILD
TENETS

1 HEALTHY
Each student enters school healthy and learns about and practices a healthy lifestyle.

2 SAFE
Each student learns in an environment that is physically and emotionally **safe** for students and adults.

3 ENGAGED
Each student is actively engaged in learning and is connected to the school and broader community.

4 SUPPORTED
Each student has access to personalized learning and is supported by qualified, caring adults.

5 CHALLENGED
Each student is challenged academically and prepared for success in college or further study and for employment and participation in a global environment.

For more about the Whole Child approach, visit
www.wholechildeducation.org.

ASCD
LEARN. TEACH. LEAD.